Guide to the
HUMAN BODY

Richard Walker

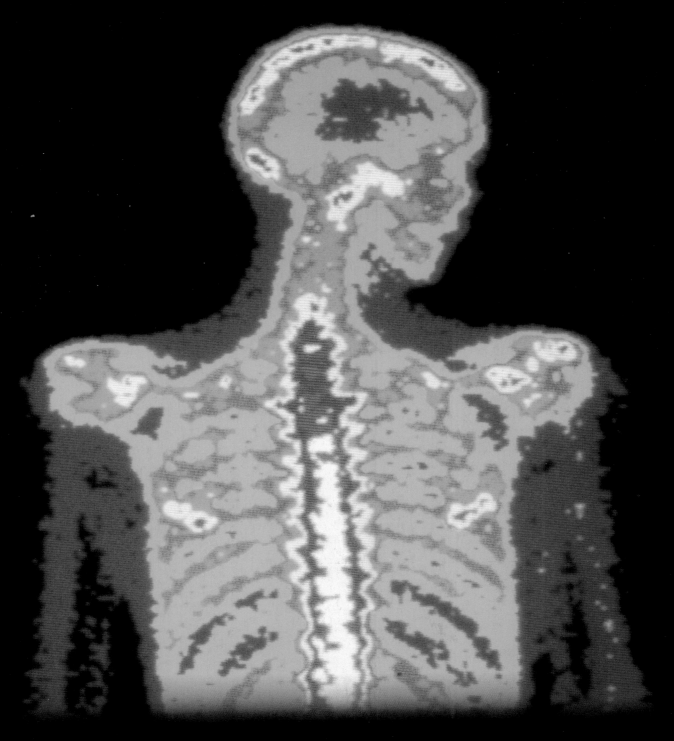

A Dorling Kindersley Book

Dorling **DK** Kindersley

LONDON, NEW YORK, SYDNEY, DELHI, PARIS,
MUNICH, and JOHANNESBURG

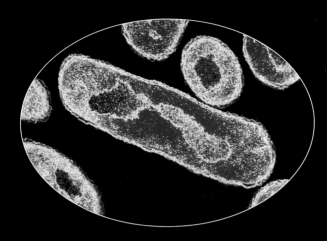

Project Art Editor Joanne Connor
Project Editor Kitty Blount
Editor Lucy Hurst
Senior Editor Fran Jones
Senior Art Editor Marcus James
Publishing Manager Jayne Parsons
Managing Art Editor Jacquie Gulliver
Photoshop Designer Robin Hunter
DTP Designer Almudena Díaz
Picture Research Samantha Nunn
Jacket Design Dean Price
Production Kate Oliver

First published in Great Britain in 2001 by
Dorling Kindersley Limited
9 Henrietta Street, Covent Garden, London WC2E 8PS

2 4 6 8 10 9 7 5 3 1

A CIP catalogue record for this book
is available from the British Library

ISBN 0-7513-3073-6

Reproduced by Colourscan, Singapore

Printed and bound by
Mondadori Printing S.p.A., Verona, Italy

See our complete
catalogue at
www.dk.com

CONTENTS

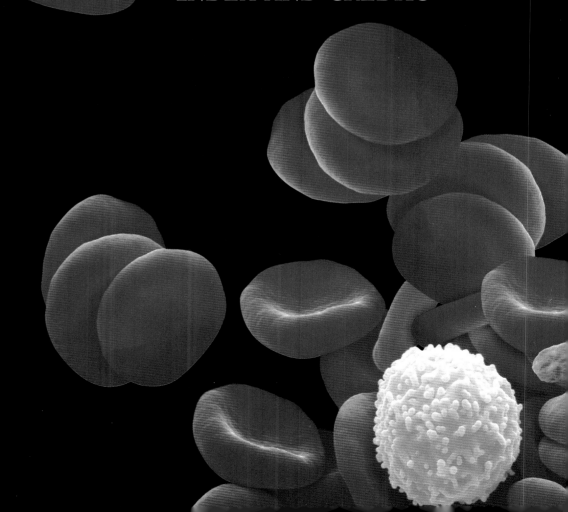

THE HUMAN BODY

Humans may look different, but inside they share identical component parts. The body's building blocks are trillions of cells. Those that perform similar tasks link together in tissue to do a specific job. There are four main types of tissue. Epithelial tissues form the skin and line hollow structures, such as the mouth. Connective tissues, such as bone and adipose tissue, support and hold the body together. Nervous tissue carries electrical signals, and muscle tissue moves the body. Tissues combine to make organs, such as the stomach, which link to form 12 systems – skin, skeletal, muscular, nervous, hormonal, blood, lymphatic, immune, respiratory, digestive, urinary, and reproductive, each with an essential role. Together, systems make a living human body.

The backbone forms the main axis of the skeleton.

Two cells separate during mitosis.

CELL DIVISION

Without cell division, growth would be impossible. All humans begin life as a single cell that divides (by a process called mitosis) repeatedly to generate the trillions of cells that form the body. When a cell divides, it produces two new identical cells. Growth ceases in the late teens, but cell division continues to replace old, worn-out cells.

LIQUID TISSUE

Each of the body's tissues are made of groups of similar cells that work together. Tissue cells produce an intercellular ("between cells") material that holds them together. In cartilage it is bendy, in bone it is hard, but in the blood it takes the form of watery plasma in which trillions of cells float. This liquid tissue transports materials and fights infection.

White blood cells are infection fighters.

Red blood cells carry oxygen.

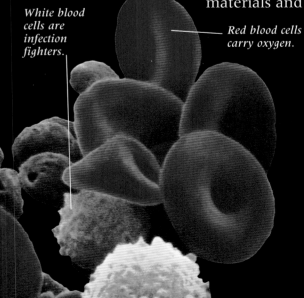

MALE BODY

The brain is the control centre of the nervous system, and enables people to think, feel, and move.

The body is made of 100 trillion (million million) cells

Kidney

Femur, or thigh bone, supports the body during walking and running.

Three billion cells die and are replaced every minute

MAJOR ORGANS

These remarkable MRI scans, which "cut" through the bodies of a man and woman, show how modern technology allows doctors to "see" inside living bodies. The major organs of several body systems can be seen here, including the long bones of the skeleton and major muscles, as well as the brain (nervous system), lungs (respiratory system), liver (digestive system), and kidneys and bladder (urinary system).

Feet bear the body's weight and help to keep it balanced.

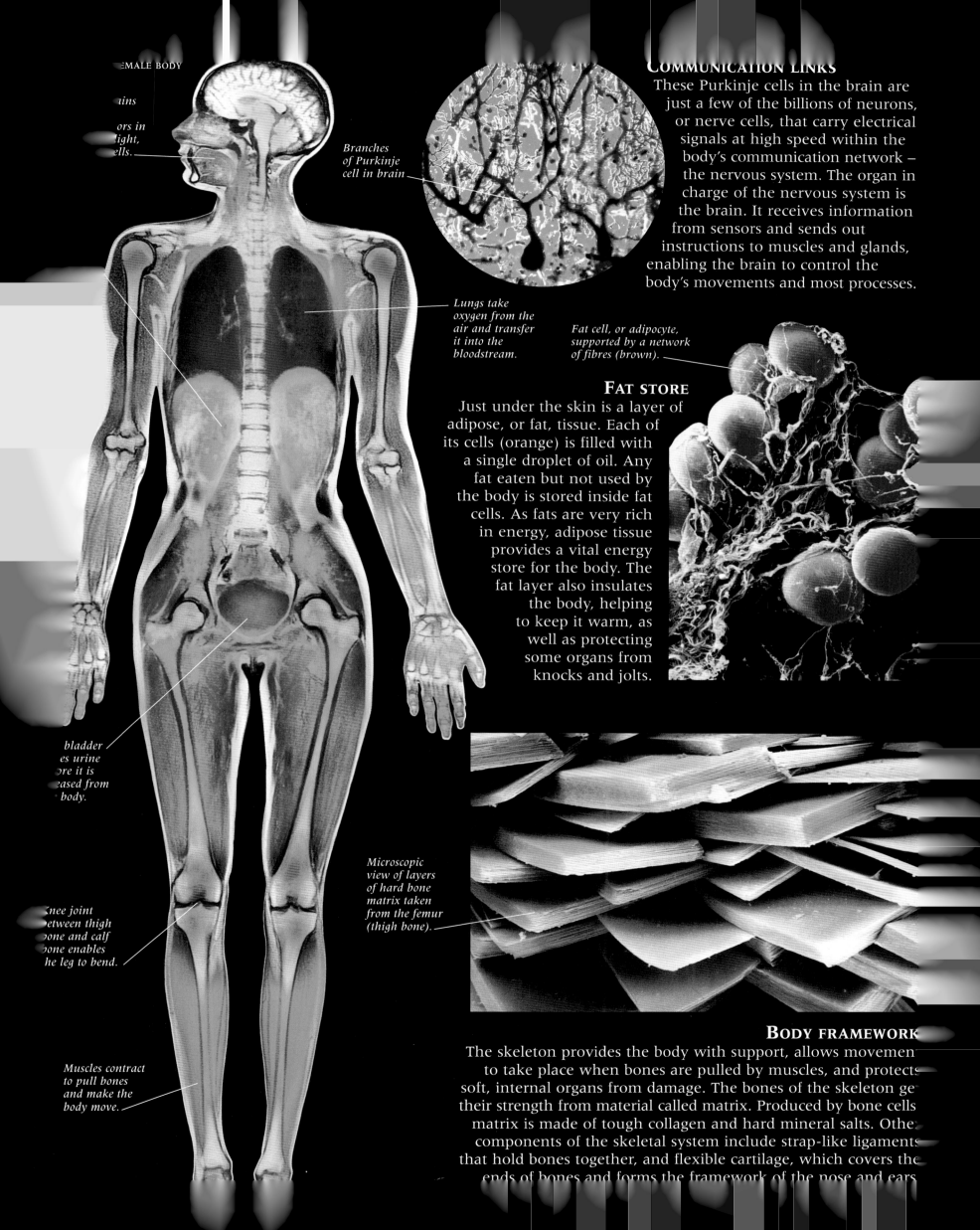

EMALE BODY

...ins

...ors in
...ight,
...ells.

*Branches
of Purkinje
cell in brain*

*Lungs take
oxygen from the
air and transfer
it into the
bloodstream.*

...bladder
...es urine
...re it is
...eased from
... body.

*...nee joint
...etween thigh
...one and calf
...one enables
...he leg to bend.*

*Microscopic
view of layers
of hard bone
matrix taken
from the femur
(thigh bone).*

*Muscles contract
to pull bones
and make the
body move.*

COMMUNICATION LINKS

These Purkinje cells in the brain are just a few of the billions of neurons, or nerve cells, that carry electrical signals at high speed within the body's communication network – the nervous system. The organ in charge of the nervous system is the brain. It receives information from sensors and sends out instructions to muscles and glands, enabling the brain to control the body's movements and most processes.

*Fat cell, or adipocyte,
supported by a network
of fibres (brown).*

FAT STORE

Just under the skin is a layer of adipose, or fat, tissue. Each of its cells (orange) is filled with a single droplet of oil. Any fat eaten but not used by the body is stored inside fat cells. As fats are very rich in energy, adipose tissue provides a vital energy store for the body. The fat layer also insulates the body, helping to keep it warm, as well as protecting some organs from knocks and jolts.

BODY FRAMEWORK

The skeleton provides the body with support, allows movemen to take place when bones are pulled by muscles, and protects soft, internal organs from damage. The bones of the skeleton ge their strength from material called matrix. Produced by bone cells matrix is made of tough collagen and hard mineral salts. Othe components of the skeletal system include strap-like ligaments that hold bones together, and flexible cartilage, which covers the ends of bones and forms the framework of the nose and ears

SKIN, HAIR, AND NAILS

T HE BODY HAS ITS OWN LIVING OVERCOAT called skin. As a protective, waterproof barrier, skin stops invading bacteria in their tracks. The brown pigment melanin colours the skin and filters out harmful ultraviolet rays in sunlight. Millions of skin sensors detect a range of sensations that include the touch of soft fur, the pressure of a heavy weight, the pain of a pinprick, the heat of a flame, or the cold of an ice cube. Hair and nails are both extensions of the skin. Millions of hairs cover most parts of the body. The thickest hairs are found on the head, where they stop heat loss and protect against sunlight. Other body hairs are finer and do little to keep the body warm – that job is done by clothes. Skin, hair, and nails all get their strength from a tough protein called keratin.

Pattern of ridges left by sweat.

FINGERPRINTS

Whenever people touch objects, especially hard ones made of glass or metal, they leave behind fingerprints. Fingerprints are copies in oily sweat of the fine ridges on the skin of the fingertips. These ridges, and the sticky sweat released onto them, help the finger to grip things. Each fingerprint, with its pattern of whorls, loops, and arches, is unique.

Nail appears pink because of blood flowing below it.

TOUGH NAILS

These hard plates cover and protect the ends of the fingers and toes. They also make picking up small objects much easier. Living cells at the root divide constantly, pushing the nail forward. As the cells move towards the fingertip, they fill with tough keratin and die. Fingernails grow about 5 mm (0.2 in) each month – faster in summer than in winter.

MICROSCOPIC VIEW OF NAIL SURFACE SHOWING FLATTENED DEAD CELLS

Tough, flat epidermal cells protect the skin below.

Cells in lower epidermis divide constantly and replace surface cells that are worn away.

About 50,000 tiny flakes drop off the skin every minute

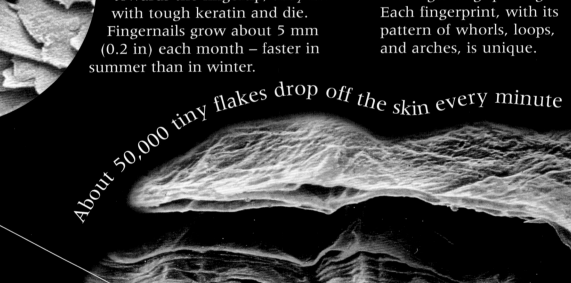

PROTECTIVE LAYERS

Skin is less than 2 mm (0.08 in) thick and has two distinct layers, as shown in this section. On top (coloured pink and red) is the epidermis. Its upper part (pink) is made of flat, interlocking dead cells, which are tough and waterproof. These cells are constantly worn away as skin flakes and are replaced by living cells in the lower epidermis (red). Underneath the epidermis is the thicker dermis (yellow). The dermis contains sensors, nerves, blood vessels, sweat glands, and hair roots.

Dermis contains sensors for touch, pressure, pain, heat, and cold.

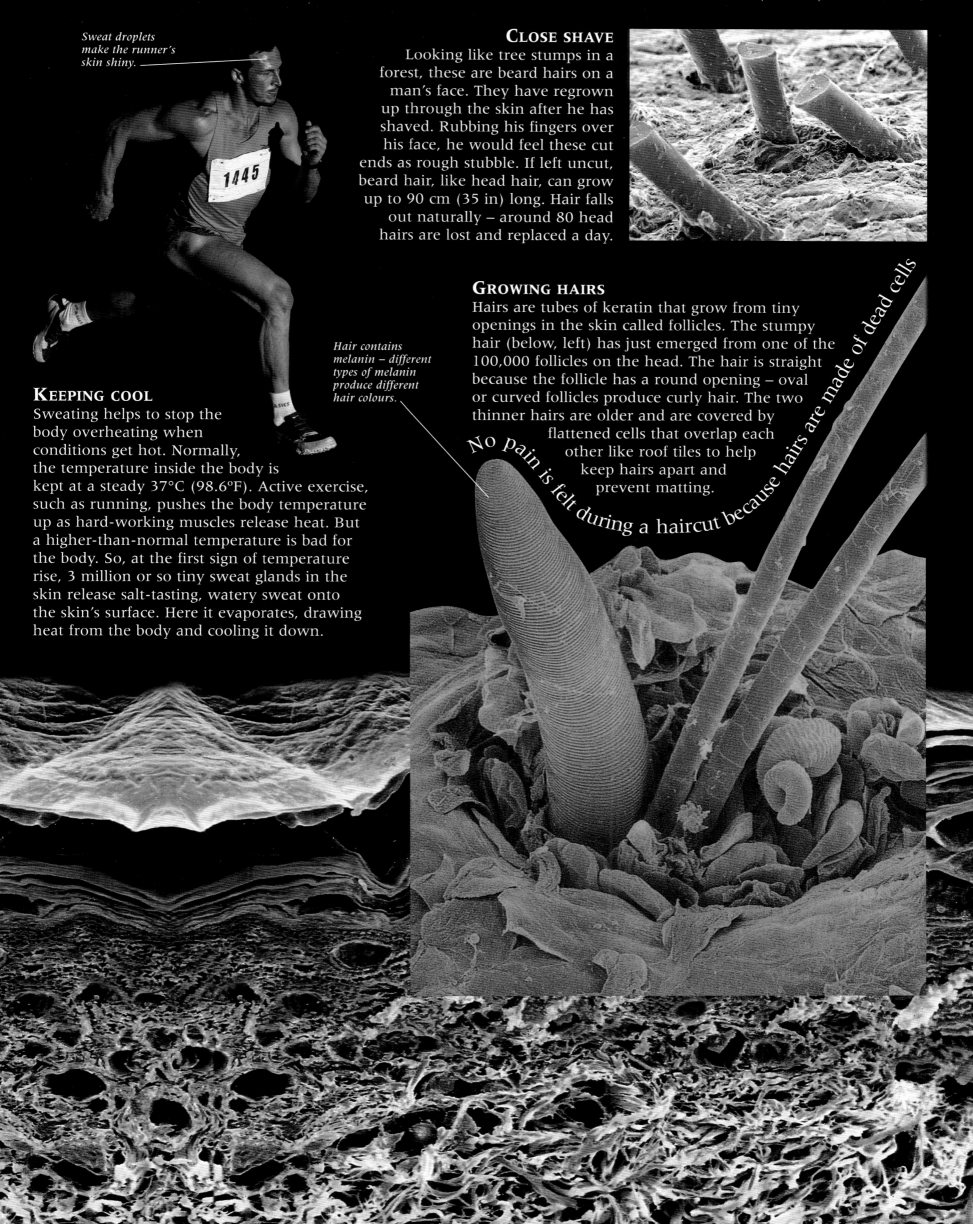

Sweat droplets make the runner's skin shiny.

CLOSE SHAVE
Looking like tree stumps in a forest, these are beard hairs on a man's face. They have regrown up through the skin after he has shaved. Rubbing his fingers over his face, he would feel these cut ends as rough stubble. If left uncut, beard hair, like head hair, can grow up to 90 cm (35 in) long. Hair falls out naturally – around 80 head hairs are lost and replaced a day.

GROWING HAIRS
Hairs are tubes of keratin that grow from tiny openings in the skin called follicles. The stumpy hair (below, left) has just emerged from one of the 100,000 follicles on the head. The hair is straight because the follicle has a round opening – oval or curved follicles produce curly hair. The two thinner hairs are older and are covered by flattened cells that overlap each other like roof tiles to help keep hairs apart and prevent matting.

Hair contains melanin – different types of melanin produce different hair colours.

No pain is felt during a haircut because hairs are made of dead cells

KEEPING COOL
Sweating helps to stop the body overheating when conditions get hot. Normally, the temperature inside the body is kept at a steady 37°C (98.6°F). Active exercise, such as running, pushes the body temperature up as hard-working muscles release heat. But a higher-than-normal temperature is bad for the body. So, at the first sign of temperature rise, 3 million or so tiny sweat glands in the skin release salt-tasting, watery sweat onto the skin's surface. Here it evaporates, drawing heat from the body and cooling it down.

SKELETON

WITHOUT ITS SKELETON, the body would collapse in a heap. The skeleton is strong but surprisingly light, making up only one-sixth of an adult's weight. It has several tasks. The framework of hard bones, bendy cartilage, and tough ligaments supports and shapes the body. Parts of the skeleton surround and protect soft, internal organs from damage. It also provides anchorage for muscles that move the body. The skeleton is often divided into two sections, each with its own roles. The axial skeleton – the skull, backbone, ribs, and sternum (breastbone) – is the main supporting core of the body, and also protects the brain, eyes, heart, and lungs. The appendicular skeleton includes arm and leg bones – the body's major movers – and the shoulder and hip bones that attach them to the axial skeleton.

Hand grips and operates computer mouse.

MOVING HANDS

Moving a computer mouse is just one task performed by the hands, the most flexible and versatile parts of the body. Flexibility is provided by the 27 bones of the wrist, palm, and fingers, seen in the X-ray above. They allow the hand to perform a wide range of movements aided by the pulling power of some 30 muscles, mostly located in the arm.

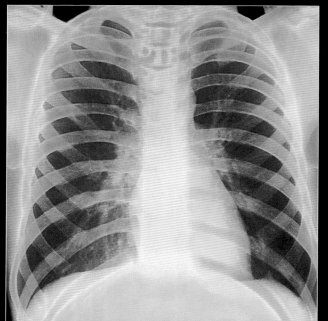

CHEST X-RAY OF AN 11-YEAR-OLD

PROTECTIVE CAGE

Twelve pairs of ribs curve from the backbone to the front of the chest. The upper 10 ribs are linked to the sternum (breastbone) by flexible cartilage. Together, backbone, ribs, and sternum create a bony cage to protect the delicate organs of the chest and upper abdomen. The X-ray (left) shows the lungs (dark blue), the heart (yellow), and their protective ribcage (pink bands).

ELBOW

FLEXIBLE FRAMEWORK

If bones were fixed together they would be ideal for supporting the body, but no good for movement. Fortunately, where most bones meet there are mobile joints that make the skeleton flexible. Movement (as shown right) can involve many different bones and joints in the feet, legs, back, arms, hands, and neck.

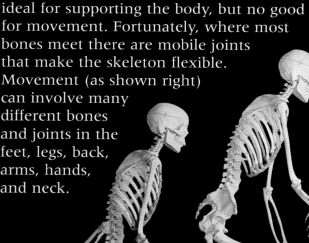

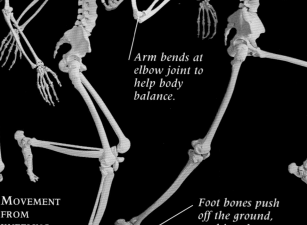

Arm bends at elbow joint to help body balance.

MOVEMENT FROM KNEELING TO RUNNING

Foot bones push off the ground, pushing the body forward.

SEEING A SKELETON

Until recently, the only way to see the body's bony framework was by X-ray. Now technology has found alternatives, such as this bone, or radionuclide, scan (left). For this procedure, a person is given a radioactive substance that is rapidly taken up by the bones. A scanner then picks up radiation given off by the bones to produce an image. Although not as clear as an X-ray, a scan gives doctors extra information. It indicates bone cell activity, and any areas of bone injury or disease.

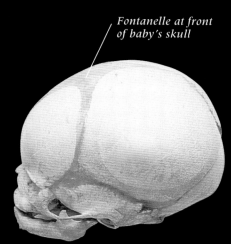

Fontanelle at front of baby's skull

SKULL

RIBS

BACKBONE

PELVIS

A newborn baby has about 350 bones, but because some fuse together as the baby grows, adults have 206 bones

BABY'S SKULL

The skull is made up of several bones locked together to form a solid structure. But when babies are born they have membrane-filled gaps called fontanelles between their skull bones. Fontanelles make the skull flexible, allowing the baby's head to be squeezed slightly during birth. It also means the skull can expand as the baby's brain grows. By the time the baby is 18 months old, the fontanelles have been replaced by bone.

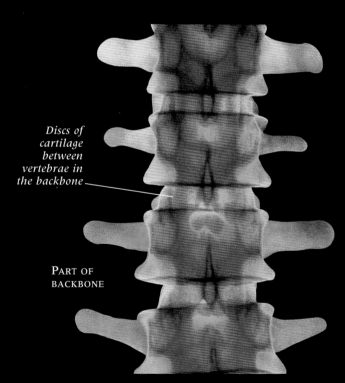

Discs of cartilage between vertebrae in the backbone

PART OF BACKBONE

CARTILAGE

The discs between backbone vertebrae are just one example of cartilage in the skeletal system. There are three types of this tough, flexible tissue. Fibrous cartilage discs make the backbone flexible and absorb shocks during running. Glassy hyaline cartilage covers the ends of bones in joints, and forms the bendy part of the nose. Elastic cartilage gives lightweight support in, for example, the outer ear flap.

RY AND LIFELESS – THE REMAINS OF PEOPLE LONG DEAD – IS how most people imagine bones. But the bones of a living person are nothing like that. They are wet, have a rich supply of blood vessels and nerves, contain living cells, are constantly reshaping and rebuilding themselves, and can repair themselves if damaged. The bone tissue, or matrix, that makes up bone has two main ingredients. Mineral salts, particularly calcium phosphate, give bone hardness. A protein called collagen gives bones flexibility, great strength, and the ability to resist stretching and twisting. Dotted throughout the matrix are the bone cells that maintain it. Bone matrix takes two forms – compact bone is dense and heavy, while honeycomb-like spongy bone is lighter. Together they make bones strong but not too heavy. Spongy bone, and the spaces inside some bones, are filled with jelly-like bone marrow. Yellow marrow stores fat, while red marrow makes blood cells.

FEMUR (THIGH BONE) PARTLY CUT OPEN

Struts called trabeculae provide strong support.

INSIDE A BONE
A bone is made up of different layers. On the outside is dense compact bone and inside this is a honeycomb layer of spongy bone. In a long bone, such as this femur (thigh bone), compact bone is thicker along the shaft, while spongy bone fills most of each end. In living femurs, the hollow centre is filled with marrow.

Weight for weight bone is five times stronger than steel

A surgeon's gloved hand holds fragments of mother-of-pearl from a giant oyster.

SPONGY BONE
As this microscopic view shows, spongy bone has a honeycomb structure of spaces and supporting struts. These struts are called trabeculae – the name means "little beams". Trabeculae are narrow, which makes spongy bone light, and they are arranged in such a way as to provide maximum resistance to pressure and stress. So, spongy bone combines lightness and strength.

BONE REPAIR KIT
Normally bones can repair themselves. But if they are shattered in an accident or badly damaged by disease, they may need some help. The silver lining of an oyster's shell, called mother-of-pearl, can stimulate bone repair. Crushed mother-of-pearl is mixed with blood or bone cells, moulded into shape, and implanted into the body. Very quickly, bone cells lay down matrix inside the implant and the bone rebuilds itself so it is just as strong as it was before.

BONE CELL
Osteocytes are bone cells that keep the bone healthy and in good condition. This microscopic cross section of bone matrix (blue) shows a single osteocyte (green). Osteocytes keep in touch through tiny threads in the matrix called canaliculi (pink). Two other types of bone cells, called osteoblasts and osteoclasts, continually reshape bones. Osteoblasts build up the bone matrix while osteoclasts break it down.

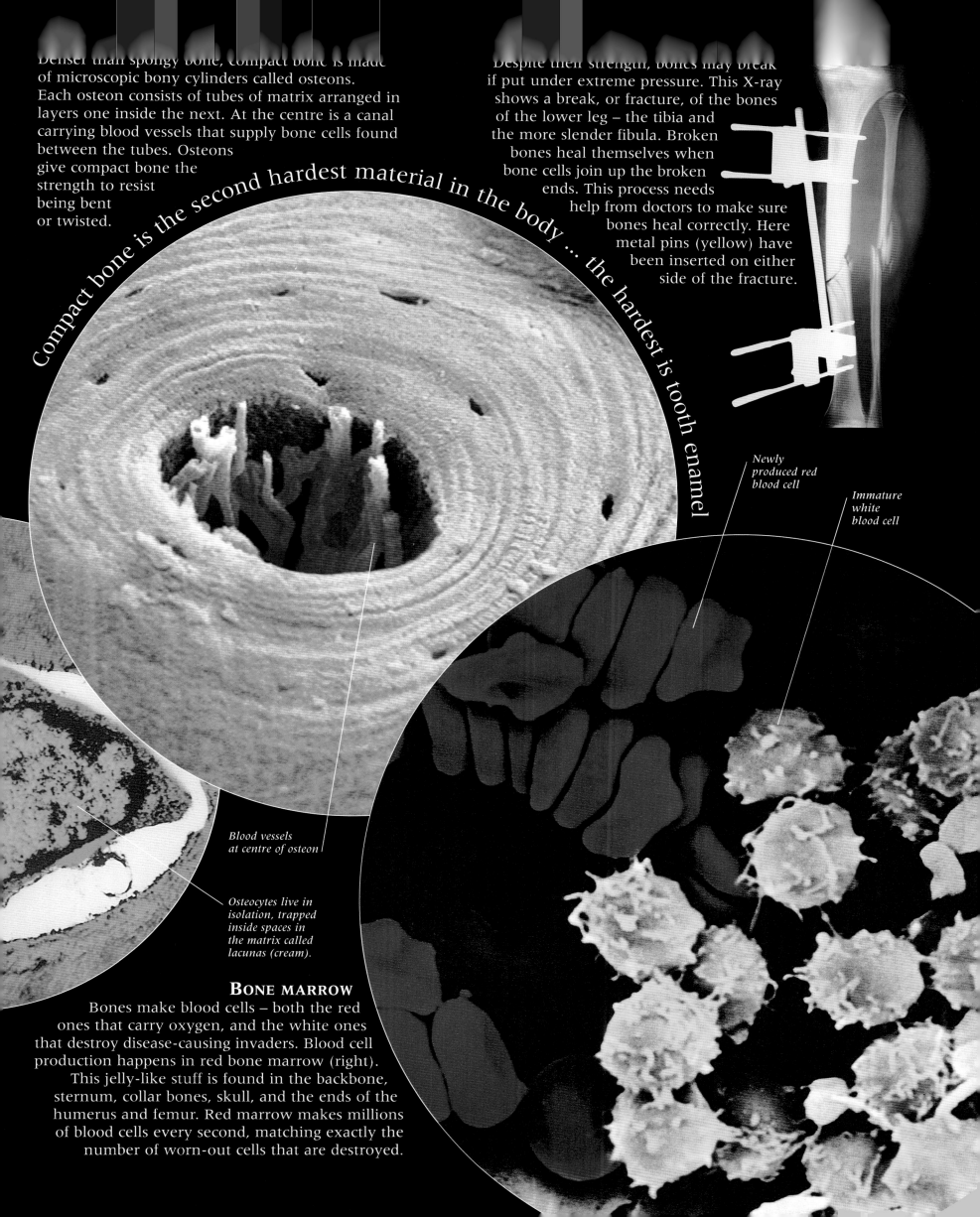

Denser than spongy bone, compact bone is made of microscopic bony cylinders called osteons. Each osteon consists of tubes of matrix arranged in layers one inside the next. At the centre is a canal carrying blood vessels that supply bone cells found between the tubes. Osteons give compact bone the strength to resist being bent or twisted.

Despite their strength, bones may break if put under extreme pressure. This X-ray shows a break, or fracture, of the bones of the lower leg – the tibia and the more slender fibula. Broken bones heal themselves when bone cells join up the broken ends. This process needs help from doctors to make sure bones heal correctly. Here metal pins (yellow) have been inserted on either side of the fracture.

Compact bone is the second hardest material in the body ... the hardest is tooth enamel

Newly produced red blood cell

Immature white blood cell

Blood vessels at centre of osteon

Osteocytes live in isolation, trapped inside spaces in the matrix called lacunas (cream).

BONE MARROW
Bones make blood cells – both the red ones that carry oxygen, and the white ones that destroy disease-causing invaders. Blood cell production happens in red bone marrow (right). This jelly-like stuff is found in the backbone, sternum, collar bones, skull, and the ends of the humerus and femur. Red marrow makes millions of blood cells every second, matching exactly the number of worn-out cells that are destroyed.

JOINTS

WHILE BONES FORM THE FRAMEWORK of the skeleton, and muscles supply the power for movement, it is joints that actually give the skeleton flexibility and allow movement to take place. Joints occur wherever two or more bones come into close contact, allowing those bones to move. A joint's usefulness becomes clear if a person tries to eat a meal without bending their elbow, or to run without bending their knees. Most joints, known as synovial joints, move freely. The six types of synovial joints include ball-and-socket, hinge, and gliding joints. Each has its own range of movements, which are determined by the shape of the bone ends and how they fit together in the joint. Partially moveable joints, such as those in the backbone, only allow a little movement. In fixed joints, such as those in the skull, no movement is possible.

Ball-and-socket joint

Femur, or thigh bone

People who are "double-jointed" don't have extra joints, just looser ligaments

Hinge joint in the knee connects the femur and tibia.

Temporal bone forms part of case around brain.

Maxilla (facial bone)

Mandible or lower jaw (facial bone)

PARTS OF THE SKULL

ADULT SKULL

Gliding joints between tarsal bones

Patellar (knee cap) ligament supports the knee as it bends.

TOUGH STRAPS

Without ligaments, joints would be very unstable. These tough straps, made of fibrous tissue, hold bones together where they meet at a joint. In the knee joint (right) both internal and external ligaments steady the joint when the knee bends, and stop the bones moving from side to side. Sometimes joints are "dislocated" when bones are wrenched out of place and ligaments tear.

KNEE JOINT

SKULL STRENGTH

The skull is very strong. It needs to be in order to support and protect the brain, house the eyes and other sense organs, and to form the framework of the face. Immoveable joints, called sutures, give the skull strength. They lock together 21 of the 22 skull bones like pieces in a jigsaw. Only the mandible, or lower jaw, moves freely to permit breathing, eating, and speaking.

GLIDING JOINT (FOOT)

MOVING LEG

The sequence above shows how different types of joints operate to lift the leg. The rounded top of the femur fits into a cup-shaped socket in the pelvis to form a ball-and-socket joint. This allows movement in many directions including upwards and out to the side. At the knee, a hinge joint allows backward and forward movement only, either bending or straightening the leg. There is also a hinge joint in the ankle, allowing the foot to be pointed up or down. Gliding joints between the tarsal bones in the ankle permit short sliding movements, making the foot strong but flexible.

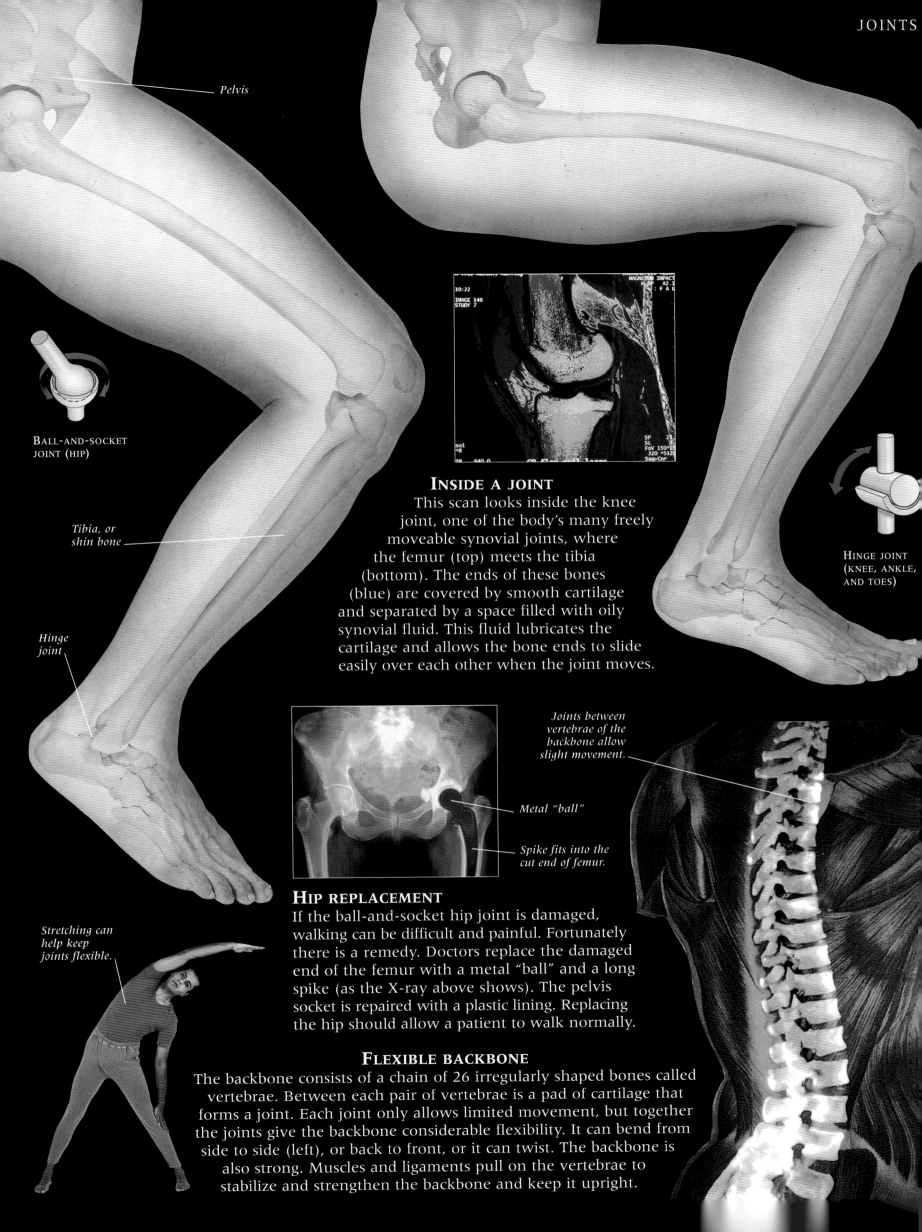

Pelvis

BALL-AND-SOCKET JOINT (HIP)

Tibia, or shin bone

Hinge joint

HINGE JOINT (KNEE, ANKLE, AND TOES)

INSIDE A JOINT

This scan looks inside the knee joint, one of the body's many freely moveable synovial joints, where the femur (top) meets the tibia (bottom). The ends of these bones (blue) are covered by smooth cartilage and separated by a space filled with oily synovial fluid. This fluid lubricates the cartilage and allows the bone ends to slide easily over each other when the joint moves.

Joints between vertebrae of the backbone allow slight movement.

Metal "ball"

Spike fits into the cut end of femur.

Stretching can help keep joints flexible.

HIP REPLACEMENT

If the ball-and-socket hip joint is damaged, walking can be difficult and painful. Fortunately there is a remedy. Doctors replace the damaged end of the femur with a metal "ball" and a long spike (as the X-ray above shows). The pelvis socket is repaired with a plastic lining. Replacing the hip should allow a patient to walk normally.

FLEXIBLE BACKBONE

The backbone consists of a chain of 26 irregularly shaped bones called vertebrae. Between each pair of vertebrae is a pad of cartilage that forms a joint. Each joint only allows limited movement, but together the joints give the backbone considerable flexibility. It can bend from side to side (left), or back to front, or it can twist. The backbone is also strong. Muscles and ligaments pull on the vertebrae to stabilize and strengthen the backbone and keep it upright.

MUSCLES

ALL BODY MOVEMENTS, from running for a bus to squeezing urine out of the bladder, depend on muscles. Muscles are made of cells that have the unique ability to contract – which means get shorter. The trigger for contraction is the arrival of nerve impulses from the brain or spinal cord. Three types of muscles are found in the body. Skeletal muscles, as their name suggests, move the skeleton. They are attached to bones across joints by tough cords called tendons. Smooth muscle is found in the walls of hollow organs such as the small intestine, bladder, and blood vessels. Cardiac muscle is found only in the wall of the heart where it contracts tirelessly over a lifetime, pumping blood around the body. It contracts automatically, although nerve impulses from the brain speed it up or slow it down according to the body's demands.

Sternocleidomastoid pulls the head forward or turns it.

Pectoralis major pulls the arm forward and towards body.

BODY MOVERS

The muscles make up nearly 40 per cent of the body's mass and, by covering the skeleton, give the body shape. Muscles occur in layers, especially in the trunk or torso. Superficial muscles, lying just under the skin, cover two or more deeper muscle layers. Some muscles are strap-like, others bulge in the middle, while some are broad and sheet-like. Most skeletal muscles are given a Latin name that relates to their shape, location, or the movement they produce.

Tibialis anterior lifts the foot during walking.

Quadriceps femoris is a group of muscles that straightens the knee.

SKELETON WITH MAJOR
SKELETAL MUSCLES OF
THE FRONT OF THE BODY

Biceps contracts to bend the arm.

Triceps contracts to straighten the arm.

WORKING IN PAIRS

Each individual muscle can only move the bones to which it is attached in one direction. To move in the other direction requires another muscle with an opposing action. This explains why muscles are normally arranged in pairs – called antagonistic pairs – with one on each side of the joint between the bones. This can be seen clearly in the arm. The biceps muscle at the front of the upper arm pulls the forearm bones upwards to flex (bend) the arm at the elbow. Its opposing number, the triceps, pulls the forearm bones downwards to straighten the arm at the elbow.

MUSCLES THAT RAISE AND
LOWER THE FOREARM

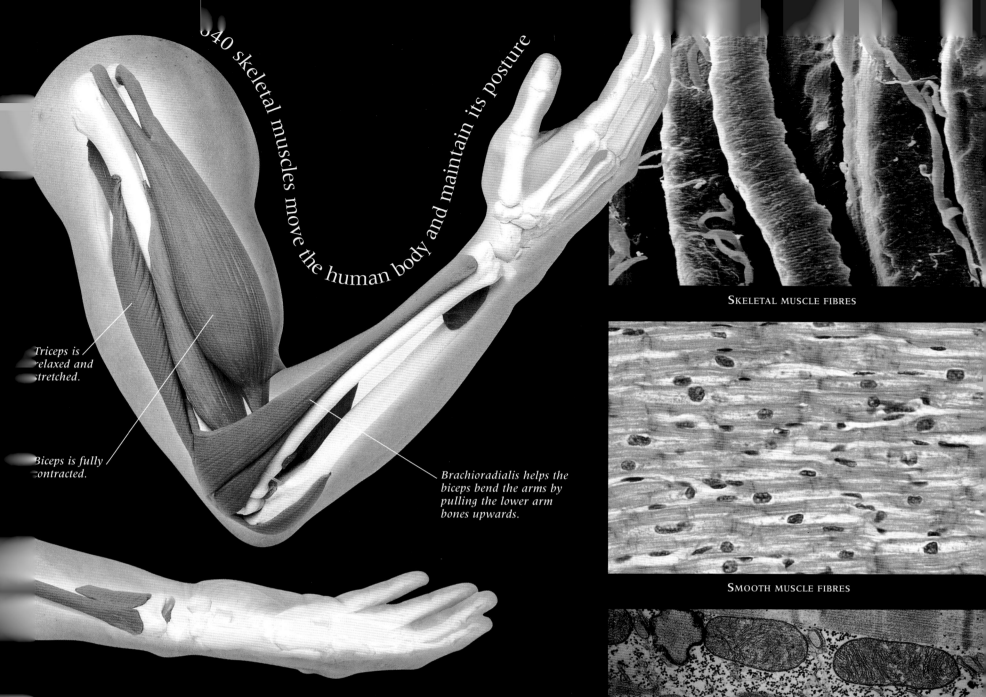

Triceps is relaxed and stretched.

Biceps is fully contracted.

Brachioradialis helps the biceps bend the arms by pulling the lower arm bones upwards.

SKELETAL MUSCLE FIBRES

SMOOTH MUSCLE FIBRES

CARDIAC MUSCLE FIBRES

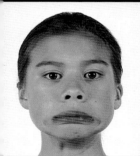
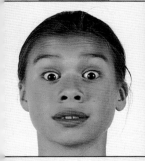

PULLING FACES
While spoken language may vary, facial expressions like these have the same meaning the world over. Disgust, surprise, and happiness are just three of the emotions that are communicated by the shape of the eyes, nose, lips, and other parts of the face. Facial expressions are produced by more than 30 muscles in the face and neck. Unlike most other skeletal muscles, these muscles pull the skin rather than moving bones.

GENERATING HEAT
Light colours in this heat photo show the areas of the body where most heat is lost during exercise. Muscles use energy-rich glucose to contract, releasing heat which is distributed by blood to warm the body to 37°C (98.6°F). Muscles work harder and release more heat during exercise. To prevent overheating, excess body heat is lost via blood vessels in the skin.

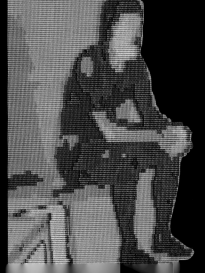

MUSCLE FIBRES
Muscles are made up of cells called fibres. The shape and size of these fibres depends on the type of muscle. The cylindrical fibres of skeletal muscle (top) can reach up to 30 cm (12 in) long. The short, tapering fibres of smooth muscle (centre) contract slowly to, for example, push food along the digestive system. The branching fibres of cardiac muscle (bottom) are found only in the wall of the heart. They contract automatically and without tiring some 100,000 times each day to pump blood around the body.

BRAIN

REMEMBERING A FACE, FEELING PAIN, solving a puzzle, or getting angry, are all made possible by the brain – the control centre of both nervous system and body. As squashy as raw egg, the pinkish, wrinkled brain sits protected within the skull. Its importance is indicated by the fact that although it makes up just 2 per cent of the body's weight it uses 20 per cent of its energy. The largest part of the brain, the cerebrum, gives people conscious thought and personality. Sensory areas of the cortex, the cerebrum's thin outer layer, receive non-stop input from sensors, such as the eyes. Motor areas of the cortex send instructions to muscles and other organs, while association areas analyze and store messages enabling people to think, understand, and remember. The brain's two other major areas are the cerebellum, which controls balance and co-ordinated movement, and the brain stem, which regulates essential functions including heart and breathing rate.

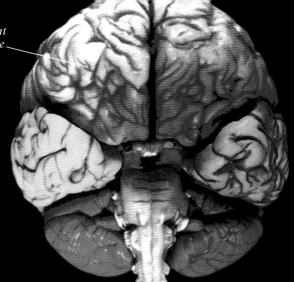

Frontal lobe of right cerebral hemisphere

BRAIN PARTS
This front view of the brain shows that it has three main parts. The largest region, the cerebrum, is divided into left and right halves, or hemispheres (dark pink and yellow). The cerebellum (green), also made up of two wrinkled hemispheres, lies at the back of the brain. The brain stem (light pink) links the brain to the spinal cord.

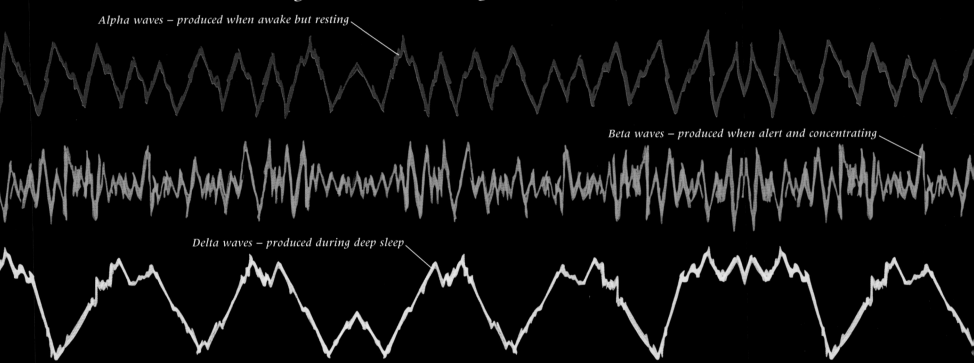

Alpha waves – produced when awake but resting

Beta waves – produced when alert and concentrating

Delta waves – produced during deep sleep

BRAIN WAVES
Every second, millions of nerve impulses flash along the brain's neurons. Tiny electrical currents produced by this endless stream of messages can be recorded as an encephalogram (EEG) – a pattern of brain waves. As a person's activity changes, so do their brain waves. Alpha waves occur when someone is awake but resting; beta waves when someone is alert and concentrating; and delta waves during deep sleep. Doctors use EEGs to check that the brain is working properly.

SLEEP
Metal plates, called electrodes, and wires carry electrical signals from this woman's head to an electroencephalograph to show how her brain activity changes as she sleeps. Normal sleep begins with a phase of deep sleep when brain activity slows, followed by light sleep when brain activity increases, the eyes move rapidly, and dreaming happens. This cycle of deep and light sleep repeats itself several times during the night. Sleep gives the brain time to rest, recharge, and sort out the events of the previous day.

INCREDIBLE NETWORK

This neuron (far left) is one of a hundred billion found in the brain. Each one has links with tens, hundreds, or even thousands of other neurons. An axon, or nerve fibre, seen here running downwards from the neuron, carries nerve impulses to other neurons. The mass of thinner neuron branches, called dendrites, receive impulses from nearby neurons. This colossal network of axons and dendrites provides a high-speed and incredibly complex communication system.

Dendrites receive messages from other neurons. The more neuron connections, the greater a person's intelligence.

Neuron

Folds and grooves in the cerebrum increase brain power by packing more brain tissue into the skull

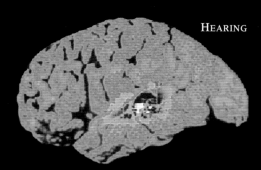

HEARING

SPEAKING

THINKING AND SPEAKING

ACTIVE AREAS

Different parts of the cerebral cortex do different jobs. This is shown by PET scans like these (above) that indicate which part is active. Hearing (top) activates an area that receives and interprets nerve impulses from the ears. Speaking (middle) involves an area further forward that sends out nerve impulses to cause sound production. Thinking and speaking (bottom) involve both the areas active in hearing and speaking, and areas for thought and understanding language.

Inner surface of right hemisphere of cerebrum

Thalamus and structures of limbic system

SCAN OF HEAD SHOWING INNER PARTS OF THE BRAIN

INSIDE THE SKULL

A CT scan of a living person's head has "removed" both the upper part of the protective skull and the left hemisphere of the cerebrum. Revealed deep inside the brain are the thalamus and structures of the limbic system. The thalamus relays messages from sensors, such as the eyes, to the cerebrum, and sends instructions in the opposite direction. The limbic system is responsible for emotions such as anger, fear, hope, pleasure, and disappointment, and works with the cerebrum to control human behaviour.

NERVES AND NEURONS

THE NERVOUS SYSTEM IS A CO-ORDINATION NETWORK that controls every thought, movement, and internal process of the body. At its core is the central nervous system (CNS) consisting of the brain and spinal cord. The CNS analyzes information arriving from the rest of the body, stores it, and issues instructions. Outside the CNS is a branching cable network of nerves that leaves the brain and spinal cord and reaches every part of the body. The nervous system is constructed from billions of linked nerve cells, called neurons, that carry electrical signals, called nerve impulses, at very high speeds. Sensory neurons carry nerve impulses to the CNS from sensors that monitor changes happening inside and outside the body. Motor neurons relay signals from the CNS that make muscles contract. Association neurons, the most numerous, are found only in the CNS. They link sensory and motor neurons, and form a complex information processing centre.

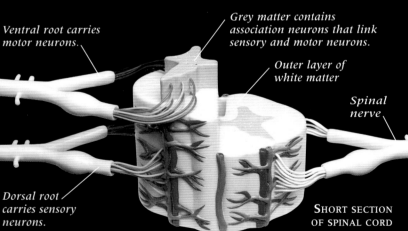

THE NERVOUS SYSTEM

FIBRE NETWORK

Neurons differ from other cells in the body in two ways. They are adapted to carrying electrical signals and parts of the cells can be very long. While the cell bodies of sensory and motor neurons lie in or near the central nervous system, their axons, or nerve fibres, can extend over long distances – up to 1 m (3.3 ft) in the case of fibres travelling from the spinal cord to the foot. Axons are bound together by fibrous tissue into nerves that resemble white, glistening cables. Most nerves are mixed – that is they carry both sensory and motor neurons.

Ventral root carries motor neurons.

Grey matter contains association neurons that link sensory and motor neurons.

Outer layer of white matter

Spinal nerve

Dorsal root carries sensory neurons.

SHORT SECTION OF SPINAL CORD

SPINAL LINK

The spinal cord is a finger-wide communication link that relays information between the brain and the rest of the body through 31 pairs of spinal nerves. Each spinal nerve splits into two roots just before it joins the spinal cord. The dorsal (back) root carries signals from the body to the spinal cord's grey matter, while the ventral (front) root transmits impulses to the muscles from the grey matter. Neurons in outer white matter carry messages up and down the spinal cord, to and from the brain.

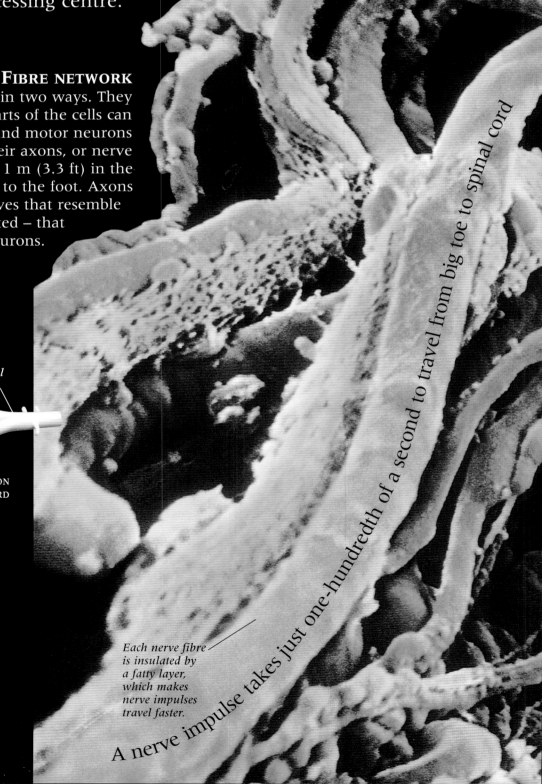

Each nerve fibre is insulated by a fatty layer, which makes nerve impulses travel faster.

A nerve impulse takes just one-hundredth of a second to travel from big toe to spinal cord

MOTOR NEURON

All neurons share the same basic structure as this motor neuron. The cell body of the neuron contains a nucleus (red) that, as in other cells, controls its activities. Branched filaments called dendrites that radiate from the cell body carry nerve impulses towards it from other neurons. The single, larger filament emerging from the top of the cell body is the axon or nerve fibre that carries impulses away.

Axon

Cell body

Dendrites relay nerve impulses to the cell body.

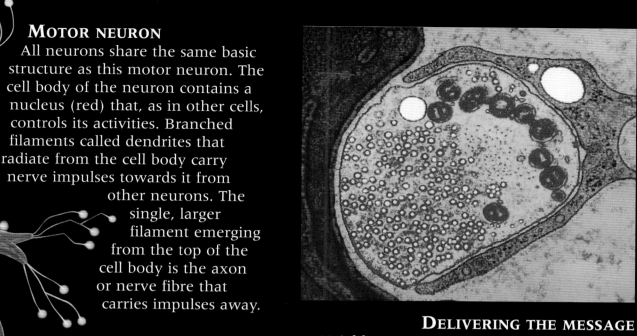

DELIVERING THE MESSAGE

Neighbouring neurons do not touch but are separated by a gap called a synapse. There is also a synapse where motor neurons and muscle fibres meet, as shown above. When a nerve impulse arrives at the end of the neuron (blue), it causes the release of chemicals, called neurotransmitters, from the inside of the neuron. These travel across the synapse and make the muscle fibre (red) contract or, in the case of neighbouring neurons, trigger a nerve impulse.

REFLEXES

The second this baby enters the water, a reflex response, called the diving reflex, closes off the entrance to her lungs so that she cannot swallow any water. Reflexes are unchanging, automatic actions that happen without a person realizing. The diving reflex disappears within months. Other reflexes that persist throughout life include the withdrawal of the hand from a hot or sharp object. Withdrawal reflexes happen very rapidly because nerve impulses are routed through the spinal cord without having to travel to the brain.

Nerve fibres run parallel to each other

EYES

VISION IS NOT ACHIEVED WITH the eyes alone, although they do play a key role. The eyes provide the brain with a constantly updated view of the outside world. More than 70 per cent of the body's sensors are found in the eyes. These light-sensitive sensors respond every time a pattern of light hits them by sending a pattern of nerve impulses to the brain along the optic nerves. The "seeing" part of vision happens when the nerve messages reach the brain, which turns them into the detailed, coloured, three-dimensional images that we actually "see". Such is the sensitivity of human eyes that they can distinguish between 10,000 different colours, and detect a lighted candle more than 1.6 km (1 mile) away.

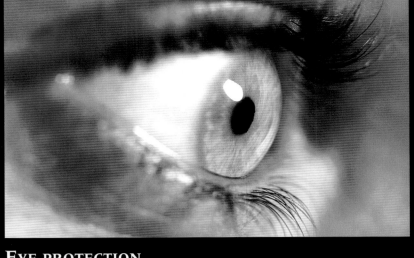

EYE PROTECTION

Eighty per cent of each eyeball is hidden inside a bony socket in the skull. But the exposed front of the eye – especially the window-like layer, called the cornea, at the front of the eyeball – needs protecting. Eyebrows stop sweat trickling down and provide shade from sunlight. Eyelashes trap irritating dust. Tears keep the front of the eyeball moist and contain germ-killing chemicals. The eyelids blink every 2-10 seconds, working like windscreen wipers to spread tears and wash away dirt. They shut instantly if an object heads towards the eyes.

CHANGING PUPILS

The pupil is a hole at the centre of the coloured iris that marks the entrance into the dark interior of the eye. Shaped like a flattened doughnut, the iris has two sets of muscle fibres. One set runs around the iris and can make the pupil contract – become smaller – while the other runs across the iris and can make the pupil dilate – become larger. Iris muscles change pupil size in a reflex action according to how bright or dim it is.

IN BRIGHT LIGHT, THE IRIS HAS MADE THE PUPIL CONTRACT TO PREVENT TOO MUCH LIGHT FROM ENTERING THE EYE.

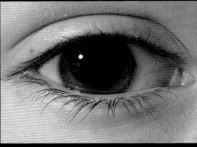

IN DIM LIGHT, THE IRIS HAS MADE THE PUPIL DILATE TO ALLOW MORE LIGHT INTO THE EYE.

RAINBOW EYES

Named after the Greek goddess of the rainbow, the iris can range in colour from the palest green in one person to the darkest brown in another. These colours are all produced by a single pigment (colouring) called melanin that is also found in skin. Irises with lots of pigment appear brown. Those with little pigment scatter light in such a way that the eyes appear green, grey, or blue.

Light scattered by pigment in the iris produces its characteristic colours.

Being interested makes a person's pupils get wider ....

The **pupil is** the opening in the centre of the iris that lets light into the eye.

This slice through a living head has been produced using a special type of X-ray called a CT scan. The eyeballs (pink) and nose are on the left, and the back of the head is on the right. Most of the space inside is taken up by the brain. The optic nerve (yellow) emerging from the back of each eyeball contains more than a million nerve fibres that carry nerve impulses at high speed to the brain. The optic nerves partly cross over before continuing to the rear of the brain.

Visual area of cerebrum receives nerve messages from retinas and turns them back into images that can be "seen".

The cornea does most of the focusing, bending light as it enters the eye.

Retina

The crystal-clear image, produced by the lens focusing light on the retina, is upside-down.

Light reflected from the tree travels to the eye.

The elastic lens changes shape to focus light clearly on the retina.

Ring of muscles around lens

....but boredom makes their pupils shrink

AN UPSIDE-DOWN WORLD

The cornea and lens focus light onto the sensors in the back of the eye. A ring of muscles around the lens can make it fatter – to focus light from nearby objects – or thinner – to focus light from distant objects. The image produced on the retina is upside-down. When the brain gets messages from the retina, it turns the image the right way up.

LIGHT SENSORS

Millions of light-sensitive cells are packed into the retina. Most are called rods (left). They work best in dim light and give black-and-white images. Other cells, called cones, enable people to see colours – but only work in a brighter light.

FLEXIBLE LENS

This microscopic view inside the lens of the eye reveals long cells called fibres arranged like the layers in an onion. Lens fibres are filled with special proteins that make them – and the lens – transparent. They also make the lens elastic so that it can change shape.

EARS AND HEARING

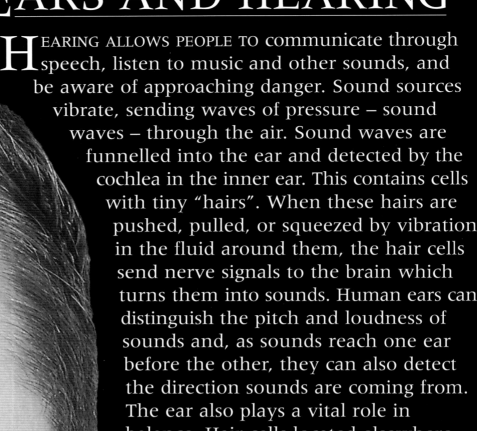

Hearing allows people to communicate through speech, listen to music and other sounds, and be aware of approaching danger. Sound sources vibrate, sending waves of pressure – sound waves – through the air. Sound waves are funnelled into the ear and detected by the cochlea in the inner ear. This contains cells with tiny "hairs". When these hairs are pushed, pulled, or squeezed by vibrations in the fluid around them, the hair cells send nerve signals to the brain which turns them into sounds. Human ears can distinguish the pitch and loudness of sounds and, as sounds reach one ear before the other, they can also detect the direction sounds are coming from. The ear also plays a vital role in balance. Hair cells located elsewhere in the inner ear constantly monitor the body's position and movements.

HIDDEN FROM VIEW

What most people identify as the ear – the external ear flap or pinna – is only a small part of it. Most of the ear is hidden from view within the skull. It has three main sections. In the outer ear is the auditory canal, kept clean and free of debris by ear wax. The middle ear links to the throat via the Eustachian tube, which ensures the air pressure is the same inside and out. The fluid-filled inner ear contains the sound and balance sensors.

Nerve carries information from balance sensors.

Semicircular canals, utricle, and saccule contain balance sensors.

Auditory canal

Middle ear

Cochlear nerve

Eardrum separates outer and middle ears.

Cochlea contains sound detectors.

Eustachian tube

EARDRUM

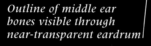

A view of the eardrum through an otoscope – the instrument that is used by doctors to look into the ear. The thin, near-transparent eardrum stretches across the end of the auditory canal, separating it from the middle ear. Sound waves channelled into the auditory canal make the eardrum vibrate.

Outline of middle ear bones visible through near-transparent eardrum

BODY LINK

No longer than a grain of rice, the stirrup, or stapes, is the smallest bone in the body and the last in a chain of three ossicles ("little bones") that extends across the middle ear. The other two ossicles are the hammer (malleus) and the anvil (incus). The ossicles transmit eardrum vibrations to the oval window – the membrane-covered inner ear opening – sending ripples through the fluid that fills the cochlea.

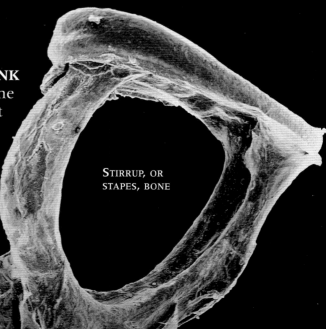

STIRRUP, OR STAPES, BONE

V-shaped sensory hairs project from hair cell.

SOUND SENSORS

The ear detects sound in the spiral organ, or organ of Corti. It runs along the centre of the fluid-filled and snail shell-shaped cochlea. Inside the spiral organ (left) are four rows of pillar-like hair cells, more than 15,000 in all, each with up to 100 sensory hairs on their upper end. Sounds arriving from the middle ear produce ripples in the cochlea's fluid that bends the hairs. This movement makes hair cells send nerve impulses along the cochlear nerve to the part of the brain where sounds are "heard".

Hair cell sends signals to the brain.

Sensory hairs inside the saccule of the inner ear

Calcium carbonate (chalk) crystal pushes or pulls on hairs depending on position of head.

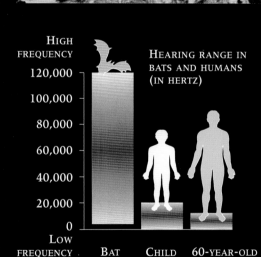

HEARING RANGE IN BATS AND HUMANS (IN HERTZ)

HIGH FREQUENCY		
120,000		
100,000		
80,000		
60,000		
40,000		
20,000		
0		
LOW FREQUENCY		
BAT	CHILD	60-YEAR-OLD

HEARING RANGE

From low-pitched growls to high-pitched squeaks, humans can detect a wide range of sounds. Pitch depends on frequency, the number of sound waves received per second, measured in hertz (Hz). Children can hear sounds between 20 Hz (low) and 20,000 Hz (high), but the upper limit decreases with age. Some animals, including bats, hear very high-pitched sounds, called ultrasounds.

Gymnast keeps her balance due to sensors in her ears and her feet.

BALANCING ACT

Balance enables people to stand up straight and move without falling. Information from balance sensors in the inner ear, and from sensors in the eyes, muscles, joints, and skin of the feet, is relayed to the brain so it "knows" about the body's position and can send nerve messages to the muscles to control the body's posture. In the inner ear, sensory hair cells in the utricle and saccule (above), monitor the head's position, while those inside the three semicircular canals detect its movements.

NOSE AND TONGUE

SMELL SENSORS ARE LOCATED in the nose and taste sensors on the tongue. Smell sensors send messages to a part of the brain responsible for emotions and remembering, which is why certain odours release feelings or memories. Taste receptors send messages to the brain's taste areas, as well as regions responsible for appetite and producing saliva. Together, smell and taste enable humans to appreciate flavours and tell the difference between hundreds of different types of food. Of the two, smell is more dominant. While the tongue can detect just four tastes, the nose recognizes more than 10,000 smells. So, if someone has a heavy cold that blocks their sense of smell, food tastes bland and flavourless. Smell and taste are also protective senses. The smell of smoke acts as an early warning to escape danger. Poisonous foods often taste bitter and can be spat out before they cause harm.

TASTE SENSATIONS

The surface of the tongue is covered with lots of tiny bumps, called papillae. Some papillae contain sensors called taste buds. As the taste map (below) shows, taste buds in different parts of the tongue are sensitive to one of the four basic food tastes – sweet, salty, sour, and bitter. Other sensors in the tongue provide the brain with information about the temperature and texture of food being chewed.

TASTE MAP OF THE TONGUE

Area sensitive to bitter taste from food such as coffee

Area sensitive to sour taste such as vinegar

Area sensitive to sweet taste such as sugar

Area sensitive to salt taste such as potato crisps

SMELL AND TASTE

This view inside the head reveals the position of the organs of smell and taste. Smell receptors are located in the olfactory (smell) epithelium that lines the upper part of the two sides of the nasal cavity. Taste sensors, called taste buds, are found on the tongue, the muscular flap that pushes food around the mouth cavity during chewing.

Thumbnail-sized patch of olfactory epithelium contains smell sensors.

Air carrying odour molecules breathed in through nostrils.

Taste sensors located on surface of tongue.

SMELL RECEPTORS

High up in the nasal cavity are more than 25 million smell receptors (right). Each receptor has, at its tip, up to 20 hair-like cilia covered in a watery mucus. Smell molecules dissolve in the mucus as they are breathed in, and then stick to the cilia. This triggers the dispatch of nerve impulses to the brain. Sniffing improves smell detection because it draws more air high up into the nose.

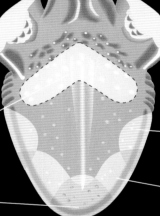

NOSE CLEARANCE

Sneezing sends a jet of mucus droplets out through the nostrils at speeds of up to 160 kmh (100 mph). This reflex action is usually triggered by infections, such as the common cold, or by irritating dust particles. A sudden blast of air through the nose rapidly clears out the irritation

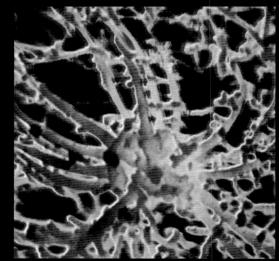

Microscopic taste sensors in the sides of the papillae on the tongue come into contact with taste molecules during chewing.

Filiform papillae are arranged in parallel rows over tongue's surface.

Papilla cut in section

TASTE BUDS

A section through papillae (right) shows some of the tongue's 10,000 taste buds. Sunk into the side of the papillae, each taste bud contains 25–40 sensory taste cells arranged like the segments in an orange. Taste hairs project from these cells into the taste pore where they are bathed in saliva when we eat. The chemicals in food dissolve in saliva and are detected by the taste hairs.

POINTED PAPILLAE

Most of the tiny bumps, or papillae, on the tongue's upper surface are cone-shaped filiform papillae. Very few contain taste buds. Instead they have touch sensors, that allow people to "feel" the food they eat, give the tongue a roughness that helps it grip and move food during chewing, and enable it to lick slippery foods such as ice cream. The tips of filiform papillae are strengthened by keratin, the tough material in nails.

Taste bud opens through pore into gap between papillae.

Dead cells, constantly worn away from surface of fungiform papillae, are replaced.

ROUNDED PAPILLAE

Dotted among the tongue's filiform papillae are rounded, flat-topped papillae (left). They are called fungiform – "fungus-shaped" – papillae because they resemble mushrooms. Taste buds are housed on the sides and around the bases of fungiform papillae, and also on 10–12 larger circumvallate papillae arranged in a V-shape at the back of the tongue. Fungiform papillae generally have a reddish colour because of the many blood vessels in the tissue that lies beneath them

HORMONES

Two SYSTEMS CONTROL AND CO-ORDINATE the body's activities. One is the fast-acting nervous system. The other, which works more slowly and has longer-lasting effects, is the endocrine system. It plays a key role in growth and reproduction, and helps control other body processes. The endocrine system consists of a number of glands that release chemical messengers, called hormones. Carried by the blood to target tissues, hormones lock onto cells and alter chemical processes going on inside them. The major endocrine glands are the pituitary, thyroid and parathyroid, and adrenal glands. Other organs that have hormone-producing "sections" include the pancreas, which also makes digestive enzymes, and the testes and ovaries, which also make sperm and eggs.

Pituitary gland

IN CHARGE
Located below the brain, the pea-sized pituitary gland is the most important part of the endocrine system, and controls most endocrine glands. At least nine hormones are released here. Some, like growth hormone and oxytocin, have a direct effect on the body. Others, like the thyroid-stimulating hormone (TSH), target other endocrine glands and stimulate them to release their own hormones.

RATE REGULATOR
This is a view (left) inside the thyroid gland, a butterfly-shaped endocrine gland found in the front of the neck just below the larynx. The red areas, called follicles, produce thyroxine. This hormone speeds up the metabolic rate of cells, that is, the rate at which their chemical reactions take place. Thyroxine production is stimulated by a pituitary gland hormone called TSH.

GROWTH HORMONE
Children and teenagers need growth hormone for normal growth and development. Released by the front lobe of the pituitary gland, growth hormone affects all body cells but it especially targets bones and skeletal muscles. It stimulates the division of cells, which causes bones and muscles to grow. Too little growth hormone in childhood means a person will be of short stature. Too much growth hormone will make someone unusually tall by the time they are an adult.

Front lobe of pituitary gland manufactures six major hormones.

Growth hormone stimulates the lengthening of long bones.

Pituitary gland cut open to show internal structure.

TWO LOBES
The pituitary gland has two parts, or lobes. The smaller back, or posterior, lobe stores two hormones produced by the hypothalamus – part of the brain. The hormones travel along nerve fibres in the stalk that links the hypothalamus to the pituitary gland. The pituitary's larger front, or anterior, lobe makes and releases the rest of the pituitary's hormones. Releasing hormones, carried by blood capillaries in the pituitary stalk from the hypothalamus to the front lobe, stimulate the production of its hormones. By controlling the pituitary gland, the hypothalamus links the nervous and endocrine systems.

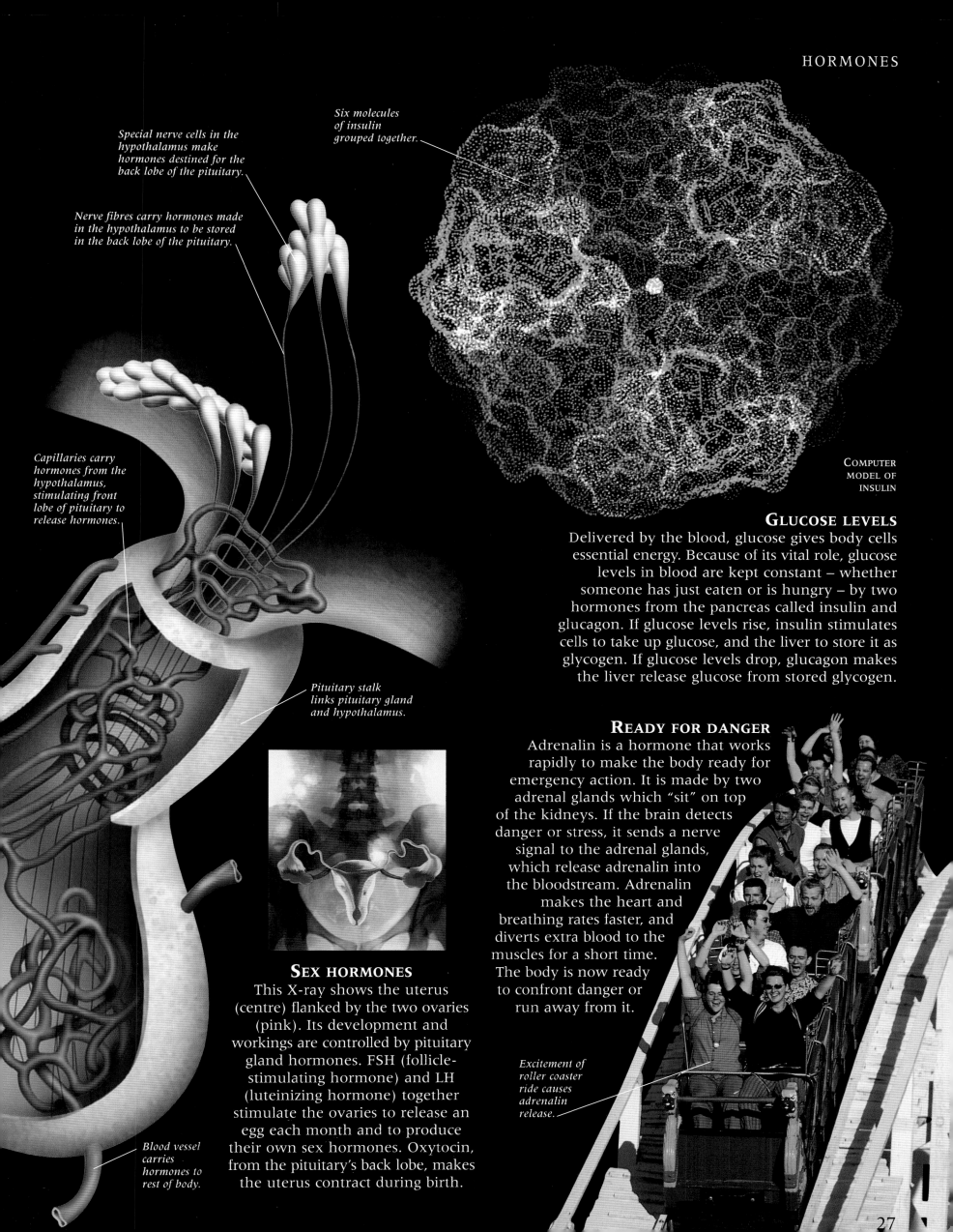

Special nerve cells in the hypothalamus make hormones destined for the back lobe of the pituitary.

Nerve fibres carry hormones made in the hypothalamus to be stored in the back lobe of the pituitary.

Six molecules of insulin grouped together.

Capillaries carry hormones from the hypothalamus, stimulating front lobe of pituitary to release hormones.

Pituitary stalk links pituitary gland and hypothalamus.

COMPUTER MODEL OF INSULIN

GLUCOSE LEVELS

Delivered by the blood, glucose gives body cells essential energy. Because of its vital role, glucose levels in blood are kept constant – whether someone has just eaten or is hungry – by two hormones from the pancreas called insulin and glucagon. If glucose levels rise, insulin stimulates cells to take up glucose, and the liver to store it as glycogen. If glucose levels drop, glucagon makes the liver release glucose from stored glycogen.

READY FOR DANGER

Adrenalin is a hormone that works rapidly to make the body ready for emergency action. It is made by two adrenal glands which "sit" on top of the kidneys. If the brain detects danger or stress, it sends a nerve signal to the adrenal glands, which release adrenalin into the bloodstream. Adrenalin makes the heart and breathing rates faster, and diverts extra blood to the muscles for a short time. The body is now ready to confront danger or run away from it.

Excitement of roller coaster ride causes adrenalin release.

SEX HORMONES

This X-ray shows the uterus (centre) flanked by the two ovaries (pink). Its development and workings are controlled by pituitary gland hormones. FSH (follicle-stimulating hormone) and LH (luteinizing hormone) together stimulate the ovaries to release an egg each month and to produce their own sex hormones. Oxytocin, from the pituitary's back lobe, makes the uterus contract during birth.

Blood vessel carries hormones to rest of body.

HEART

ONCE BELIEVED TO BE THE CENTRE for feelings of love, the heart actually has the less exciting but vital role of pumping blood. The heart lies in the chest, flanked by the lungs and protected by the ribcage. Its walls are made of cardiac muscle which contracts repeatedly without tiring. The right side of the heart pumps blood to the lungs to be refreshed with oxygen, while the left side pumps this blood to the body's cells. A single heartbeat has distinct phases. Initially, the heart relaxes, drawing blood in. Then the two ventricles – lower chambers of each side – contract together, sending blood to the lungs or body. Valves ensure the one-way flow of blood, and produce the sounds that can be heard with a stethoscope when they slam shut. At rest, the heart contracts some 70 times each minute. During exercise, heart rate increases to pump extra blood to the muscles.

The heart beats about 3 billion times in a lifetime...

Left coronary artery divides into two.

Right coronary artery

Heart lies slightly to the left of the breastbone and is tilted towards the left side of the body.

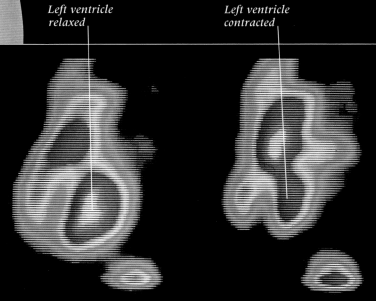

Left ventricle relaxed

Left ventricle contracted

...without ever stopping to rest

BLOOD SUPPLY

The cardiac muscle cells in the wall of the heart need a constant supply of oxygen, just like all other body cells. But the blood flowing through the chambers of the heart does not seep into the walls to supply cells with the necessary oxygen. Instead, the heart has its own blood system, called the coronary system, that keeps it working. This angiogram (above) shows left and right coronary arteries branching off the aorta, supplying both the front and back of the heart. Blood is then collected by a large vein that empties into the right atrium.

BEATING HEART

A gamma camera scan like this (above) enables doctors to watch a heartbeat in action. The camera detects red blood cells tagged with a radioactive tracer, and shows how the distribution of blood changes during the heartbeat cycle. On the left, the left ventricle is relaxed and filling up with blood. On the right, the left ventricle has contracted and contains little blood.

INSIDE THE HEART

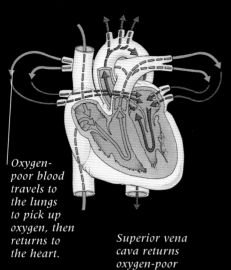

As shown left and below, each side of the heart has two linked chambers – an upper atrium, and lower, larger ventricle. Oxygen-poor blood (blue) enters through the right atrium and is pumped by the right ventricle along the pulmonary arteries to the lungs, where it collects oxygen. Oxygen-rich blood (red) returns along the pulmonary veins to the left atrium, and is pumped by the strong left ventricle to the rest of the body.

Oxygen-poor blood travels to the lungs to pick up oxygen, then returns to the heart.

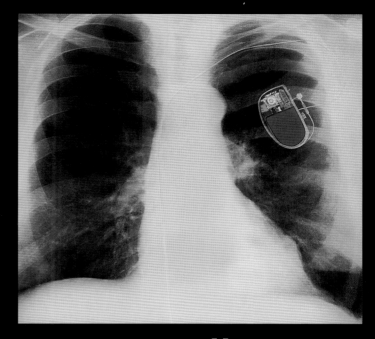

MAKING THE PACE

The heart has its own pacemaker in the right atrium wall that sends out electrical impulses triggering each heartbeat. If the pacemaker fails, doctors can replace it with an artificial version. Powered by a long-life battery, the artificial pacemaker is implanted under the skin of the chest, as seen in this X-ray. A wire carries electrical impulses to the heart. Some pacemakers send impulses at a fixed rate, others only send them if a heartbeat is missed, or the heart slows.

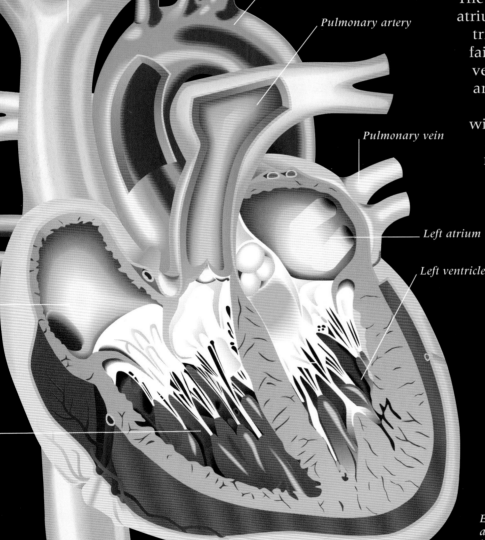

Superior vena cava returns oxygen-poor blood from the upper body to the heart.

Aorta

Pulmonary artery

Pulmonary vein

Left atrium

Left ventricle

Right atrium

Right ventricle

Inferior vena cava returns oxygen-poor blood from the lower body to the heart.

EXIT VALVE

The semilunar valve above is open to let blood exit the right ventricle along the pulmonary artery. There is an identical valve in the aorta where it leaves the left ventricle. Like other heart valves, semilunar valves maintain a one-way flow of blood. When the ventricle contracts the valve opens to let blood out. When the ventricle relaxes, its three flaps fill with blood and close the valve, stopping backflow into the ventricle.

Edge of valve attached to heart string

HEART STRINGS

Between each atrium and ventricle, a one-way valve lets blood flow into the relaxed ventricle, but closes as the ventricle contracts. These narrow cords (right), called heart strings, anchor the valve's flaps to projections on the ventricle wall. They stop the valve turning inside out – like an umbrella in a gale – when the ventricle contracts.

The biggest artery – the aorta – is 2,500 times wider than the smallest capillaries

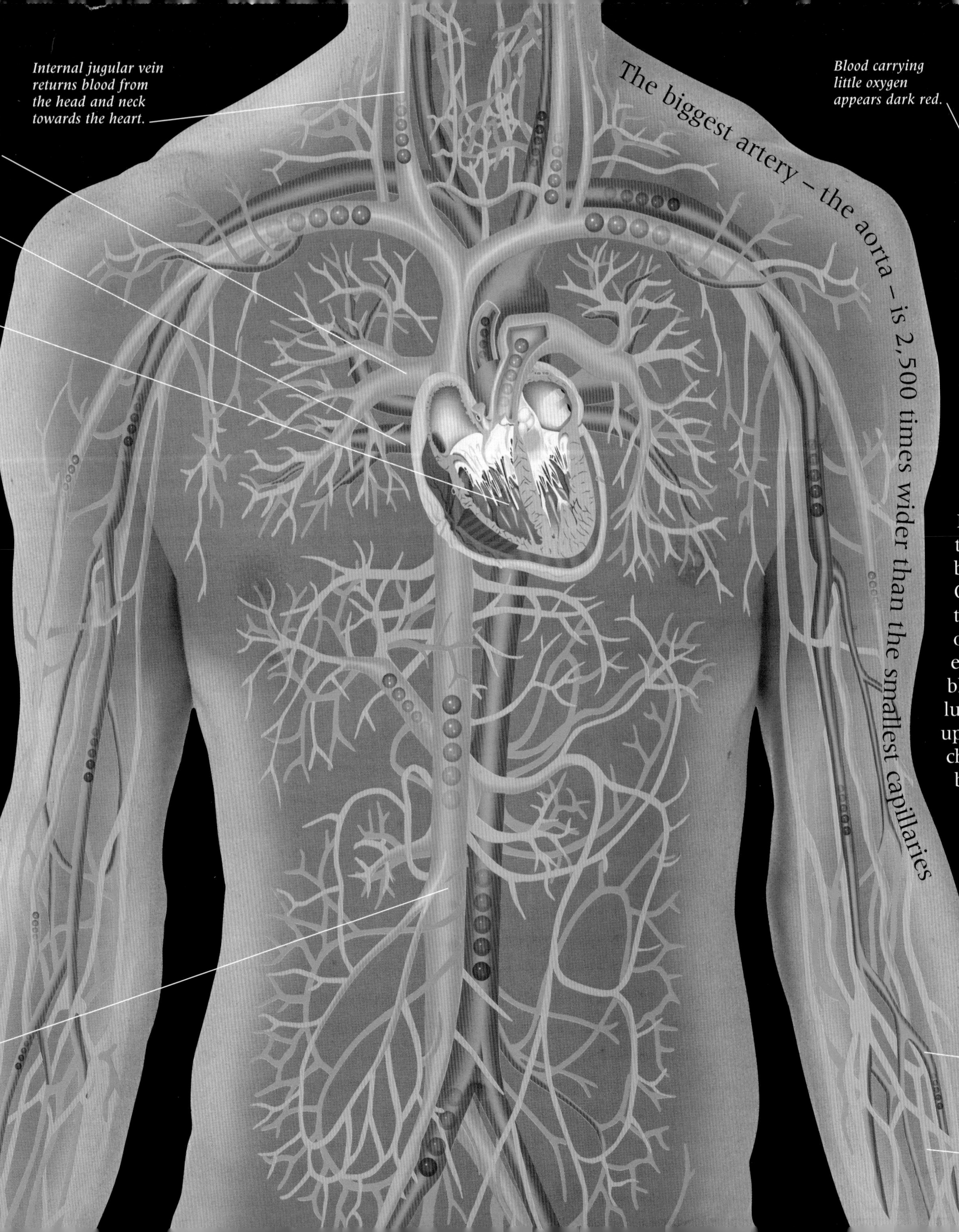

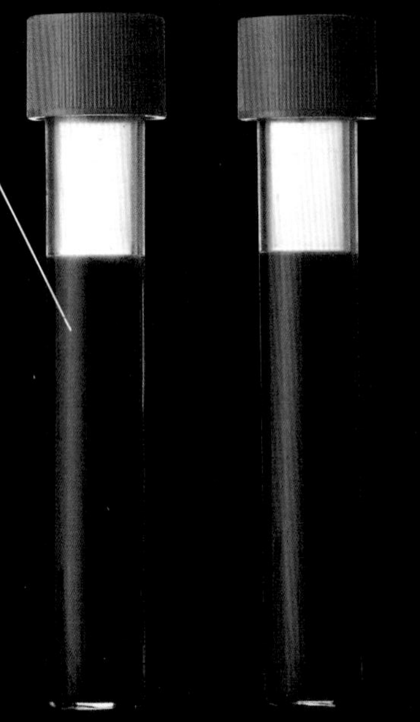

CHANGING COLOUR

Blood owes its red colour to the trillions of red blood cells that it carries. Or more specifically, to the 250 million molecules of haemoglobin within each red blood cell. When blood passes through the lungs, haemoglobin picks up oxygen. As it does so, it changes shape and becomes bright red, as does the blood. In the tissues, where demand is high, haemoglobin unloads its oxygen, changes shape once again, and makes the blood appear dark, purplish-red.

OXYGEN-POOR BLOOD

OXYGEN-RICH BLOOD

Blood carrying little oxygen appears dark red.

Oxygen-rich blood (red)

Oxygen-poor blood (blue)

MAJOR BLOOD VESSELS

Blood vessels form a branching network that reaches all parts of the body, as this "map" of the major blood vessels shows. Arteries fan out from the heart. Most deliver oxygen-rich blood (red) to the head, trunk, and limbs. The pulmonary artery is an exception. It carries oxygen-poor blood a short distance to the lungs to pick up oxygen and disposes of carbon dioxide. Veins converge to carry blood, usually oxygen-poor (blue), back to the heart. The pulmonary veins carry oxygen-rich blood from the lungs to the heart. Linking arteries and veins, but too small to be seen here, are the capillaries.

Pulmonary arteries carry oxygen-poor blood from the right side of the heart to the lungs.

Pulmonary veins carry oxygen-rich blood from the lungs to the left side of the heart.

The heart – shown here cut open – is a muscular pump that propels blood around the circulatory system.

Internal jugular vein returns blood from the head and neck towards the heart.

Inferior vena cava is the main vein carrying blood from the abdomen and legs to the right side of the heart.

In one drop of blood... there are 250 million red cells, 16 million platelets, and only 375,000 white cells

BLOOD

MOST PEOPLE only think about blood if they cut themselves. But this life-giving liquid flows continuously past every cell in the body. Blood keeps the body working normally by making sure that its cells are kept in warm, constant surroundings. It does that in three ways. As a transporter, it delivers food, oxygen, and other essentials, and removes waste. As a regulator, it distributes heat, keeping the body's temperature at 37°C (98.6°F). As a defender, it helps protect the body against diseases. Blood has two main components: liquid plasma and blood cells. The three types of blood cells – red blood cells, white blood cells, and platelets – are all made inside bones.

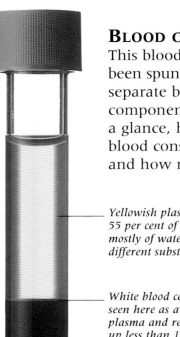

BLOOD COMPONENTS
This blood sample has been spun at high speed to separate blood's two main components. It shows, at a glance, how much of blood consists of plasma and how much of cells.

Yellowish plasma makes up about 55 per cent of blood. Plasma consists mostly of water, in which many different substances are dissolved.

White blood cells and platelets – seen here as a thin pale line between plasma and red blood cells – make up less than 1 per cent of blood.

Red cells, far more numerous than white cells or platelets, make up about 44 per cent of blood.

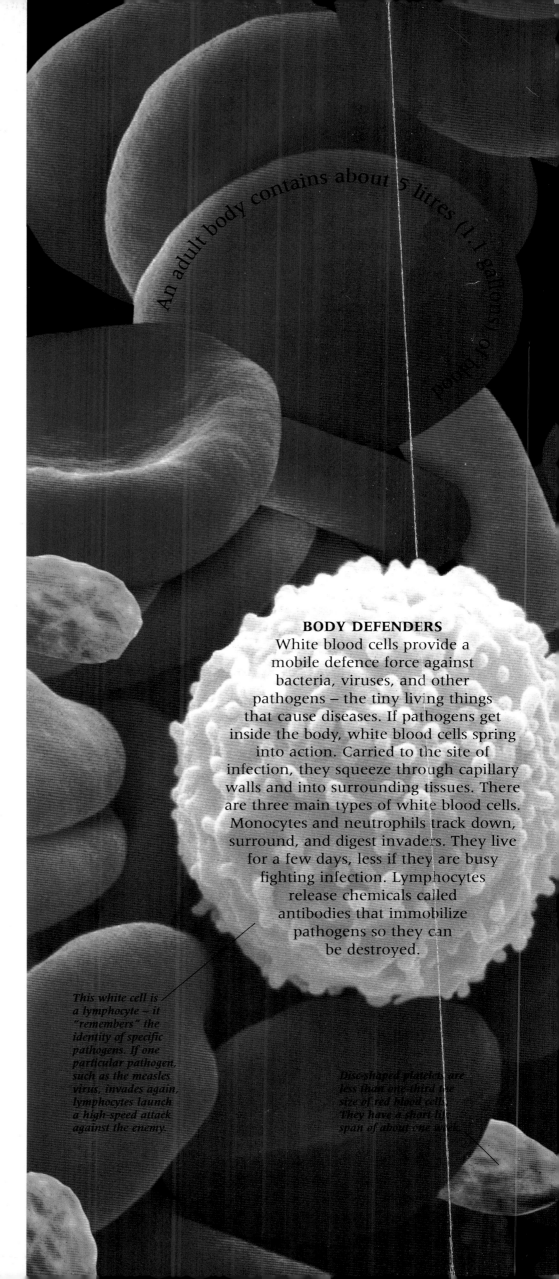

An adult body contains about 5 litres (1.1 gallons) of blood

BODY DEFENDERS
White blood cells provide a mobile defence force against bacteria, viruses, and other pathogens – the tiny living things that cause diseases. If pathogens get inside the body, white blood cells spring into action. Carried to the site of infection, they squeeze through capillary walls and into surrounding tissues. There are three main types of white blood cells. Monocytes and neutrophils track down, surround, and digest invaders. They live for a few days, less if they are busy fighting infection. Lymphocytes release chemicals called antibodies that immobilize pathogens so they can be destroyed.

This white cell is a lymphocyte – it "remembers" the identity of specific pathogens. If one particular pathogen, such as the measles virus, invades again, lymphocytes launch a high-speed attack against the enemy.

Disc-shaped platelets are less than one-third the size of red blood cells. They have a short life span of about one week.

CIRCULATION

UNTIL ABOUT 400 YEARS AGO, PEOPLE didn't really understand how blood moved inside the body, or what the role of the heart was. Previously, it was believed that blood "ebbed and flowed" along blood vessels, rather like tides at the seaside. Then, in 1628, William Harvey – an English doctor – challenged old ideas by proposing that the heart pumped blood in a one-way circuit around the body along blood vessels. Harvey's discovery provided the basis for the modern understanding of the circulatory, or cardiovascular, system. This system consists of the heart and blood vessels, together with the blood that travels through them. Its roles include conveying oxygen and food to all body cells and removing their waste products, as well as carrying specialized cells that help protect the body from disease.

CIRCULATION SYSTEM

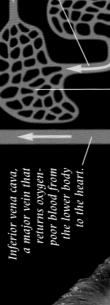

Head receives oxygen-rich blood through the carotid arteries.

Aorta, a major artery that carries oxygen-rich blood from the heart towards tissues.

Pulmonary circulation carries blood between the heart and lungs.

Lung

Heart

Hepatic portal vein carries food-rich blood from intestines to the liver.

Intestines

Liver

Inferior vena cava, a major vein that returns oxygen-poor blood from the lower body to the heart.

Lower body

DOUBLE CIRCULATION

The diagram (above) shows the route blood takes as it is pumped by the heart to the tissues and back to the heart. The body has two circulation circuits linked by the heart.

The pulmonary ("lung") circuit carries blood from the right side of the heart to the lungs to pick up oxygen, then returns oxygen-rich blood to the left side of the heart. The systemic ("body") circuit carries oxygen-rich blood from the left side of the heart to the rest of the body, and returns oxygen-poor blood to the right side of the heart.

BLOOD CLOTTING

The circulatory system has its own built-in mechanism to repair damaged blood vessels. If a vessel is cut, torn, or otherwise damaged, cell fragments called platelets stick together to help plug the hole. In addition, these "sticky" platelets, and chemicals released by the damaged blood vessel, trigger the conversion of the protein fibrinogen – which is dissolved in blood plasma – into fibres of fibrin. These fibres form a net that traps red blood cells and debris, and binds them into a clot, preventing blood from leaking out of the vessel.

Red blood cell caught in fibrin net

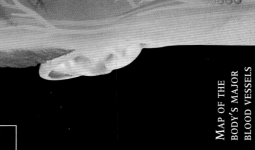

MAP OF THE BODY'S MAJOR BLOOD VESSELS

LIQUID CARRIER

Watery plasma makes blood liquid and contains more than 100 dissolved substances. Plasma plays a key part in blood's 24-hour delivery and removal service. It delivers food, such as sugars (for energy) and amino acids (for growth and repair), to every cell. It removes poisonous wastes, such as carbon dioxide. It carries chemical messengers called hormones that regulate the way cells work. Plasma proteins include germ-killing antibodies and clot-making fibrinogen.

Red blood cells are doughnut-shaped because, unlike other body cells, they have no nucleus. This leaves more space to pack in haemoglobin, a substance that carries oxygen and gives the cells their red colour.

OXYGEN TRANSPORTERS

Red blood cells are ideally suited to deliver oxygen. The haemoglobin they contain has a remarkable ability. As red blood cells make their one-minute round trip around the body, haemoglobin picks up oxygen where there is plenty of it – in the lungs – and unloads oxygen where there is little of it – around the body's cells, which greedily consume it and constantly demand more. Also, their unique dimpled shape provides a large surface through which oxygen can be very quickly picked up or unloaded. After a life span of 120 days, having travelled around the body some 170,000 times, a red blood cell is worn out, inefficient, and surplus to requirements. It is dismantled in the spleen and liver, and the useful parts are recycled.

PLUGS

Platelets are cell fragments, not complete blood cells. Their job is to help protect the body by stopping blood from leaking out of damaged blood vessels. If a hole appears, platelets stick together to plug it. They also cause the blood to clot, or thicken at that spot, and stop it spilling out.

Every second, 2 million red blood cells are made...

...and the same number are destroyed.

ROBOT CONTROL

This small object may have a role in medicine of the future. It is a prototype miniature "submarine" travelling along a blood vessel. As the technology develops, it should be possible to equip the craft with probes, sensors, and repair kits so it becomes a nanorobot, or tiny robot. Nanorobots would be used to detect and repair any defects in the circulatory system. If a blood vessel was blocked, for example, the nanorobot would be injected into the bloodstream so it could find and remove the blockage, and restore normal blood flow.

A tiny propeller powers this early version of the microscopic nanorobots that may, one day, explore the circulatory system to find defects.

Dorsal digital veins collect oxygen-poor blood from the toes.

DEEP AND SUPERFICIAL

The blood vessels of the circulatory system do not run at a fixed distance beneath the skin. As this view (above) of the lower leg shows, they and their branches pass around bones as they travel to their destination. Some, especially larger arteries and veins, are deep, passing under or between muscles and close to bones. Others, like the great saphenous vein, are superficial, passing close to the surface of the skin.

Anterior tibial artery supplies blood to the muscles at the front of the lower leg.

Posterior tibial artery passes behind the tibia and supplies the muscles at the rear of the calf that point the foot downwards.

Tibia

MAJOR ARTERIES AND VEINS SUPPLYING LOWER LEG AND FOOT

Red blood cells are the most numerous cells in the body, with more than

BLOOD VESSELS

THE BODY'S CELLS ARE supplied with blood by a network of living pipes called blood vessels which range in size from finger-thick to microscopic. There are three types. Arteries carry oxygen-rich blood away from the heart. Their walls are strong and elastic, so they expand and recoil as the heart pumps high-pressure blood along them. Where an artery passes near the skin's surface, over a bone, the surge of blood can be felt as a pulse. Tiny capillaries, the most numerous blood vessels, are branches of the smallest arteries. They fan out through the tissues, supplying cells with food and oxygen. The third type of blood vessel – veins – carry oxygen-poor blood back to the heart. They have thinner walls because they carry low-pressure blood.

FLOWING RED
BLOOD CELLS

Branches of the internal carotid artery

SEEING ARTERIES

X-rays do not usually show blood vessels. However, by using angiography, an X-ray technique in which a special chemical is injected into blood vessels, they can be easily seen. This angiogram of a side view of the head shows the internal carotid artery and its branches supplying the brain with blood. Doctors use angiograms like these to look for any signs of blockage or disease.

ARM AND HAND CIRCULATION

The radial artery and cephalic vein are just two of the arteries (red) and veins (blue) which circulate blood through the arm and hand. The radial artery travels from the elbow along the radius to the wrist where it branches into smaller arteries that supply blood to the fingers. Veins from the back of the hand drain into the cephalic vein which coils around the radius to the elbow, then continues up to the shoulder.

Radial artery

Cephalic vein

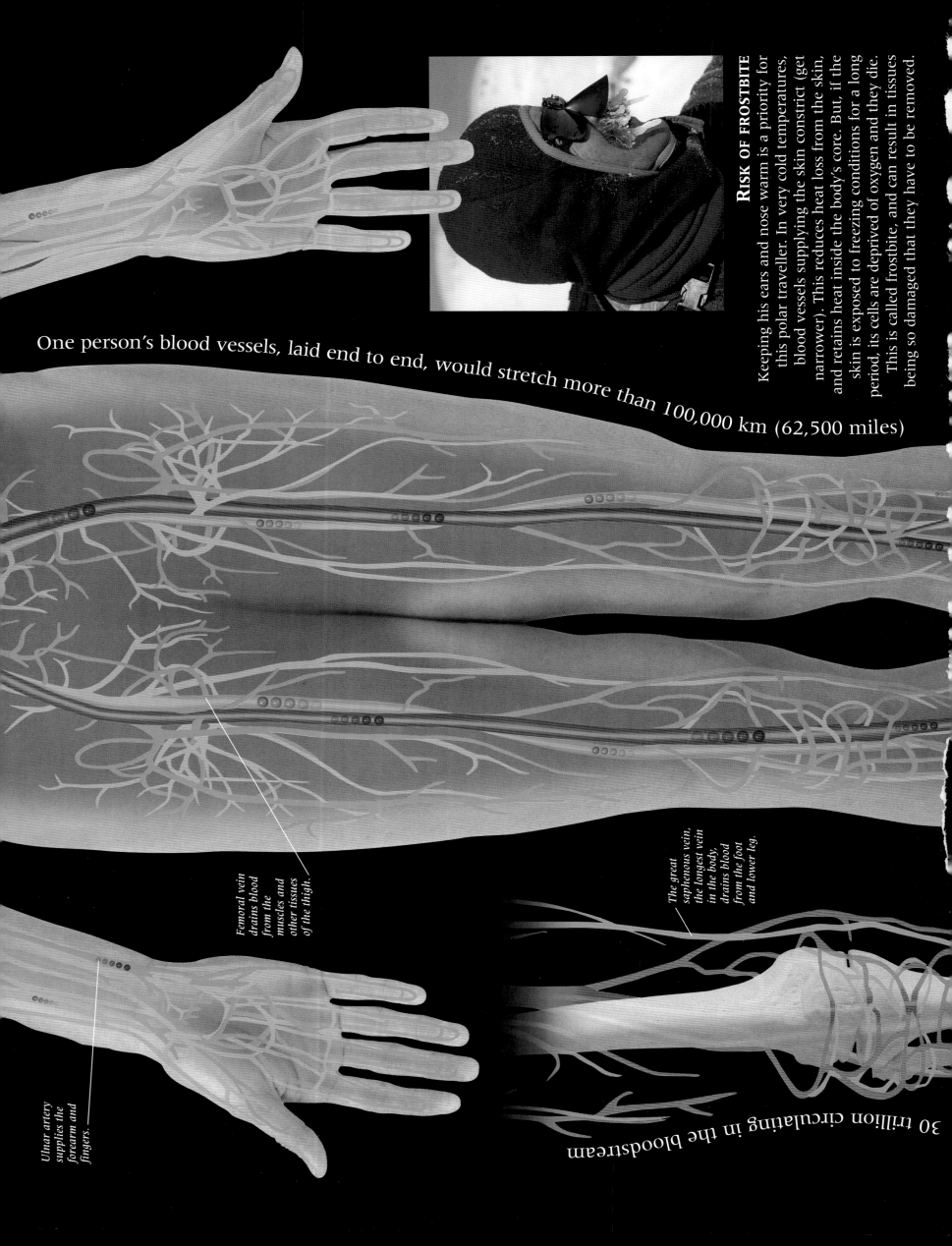

One person's blood vessels, laid end to end, would stretch more than 100,000 km (62,500 miles)

Femoral vein drains blood from the muscles and other tissues of the thigh.

The great saphenous vein, the longest vein in the body, drains blood from the foot and lower leg.

Ulnar artery supplies the forearm and fingers.

30 trillion circulating in the bloodstream

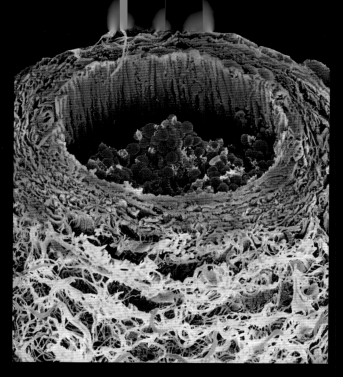

DELIVERY SERVICE

If arteries and veins are the highways of the circulatory system, capillaries are its side roads. Capillaries provide all body cells with a delivery service. Many are so narrow that red blood cells have to queue and bend to squeeze through them. Capillary walls are just one cell thick. Fluid carrying food and oxygen leaks from the blood through these thin walls, and surrounds and supplies cells, before picking up their waste and returning to the capillary.

Red blood cells queue up to pass along a capillary.

SMALLEST ARTERIES

This cross-section (above) reveals the structure of an arteriole – the smallest artery branch. The inner lumen or cavity – here filled with red blood cells – has a smooth lining that allows blood to flow easily. Surrounding this is a thicker layer of muscle (pink) that makes the arteriole wider or narrower, controlling blood flow to the tissues. The outer layer (yellow) protects the arteriole. Arterioles branch to form even narrower capillaries.

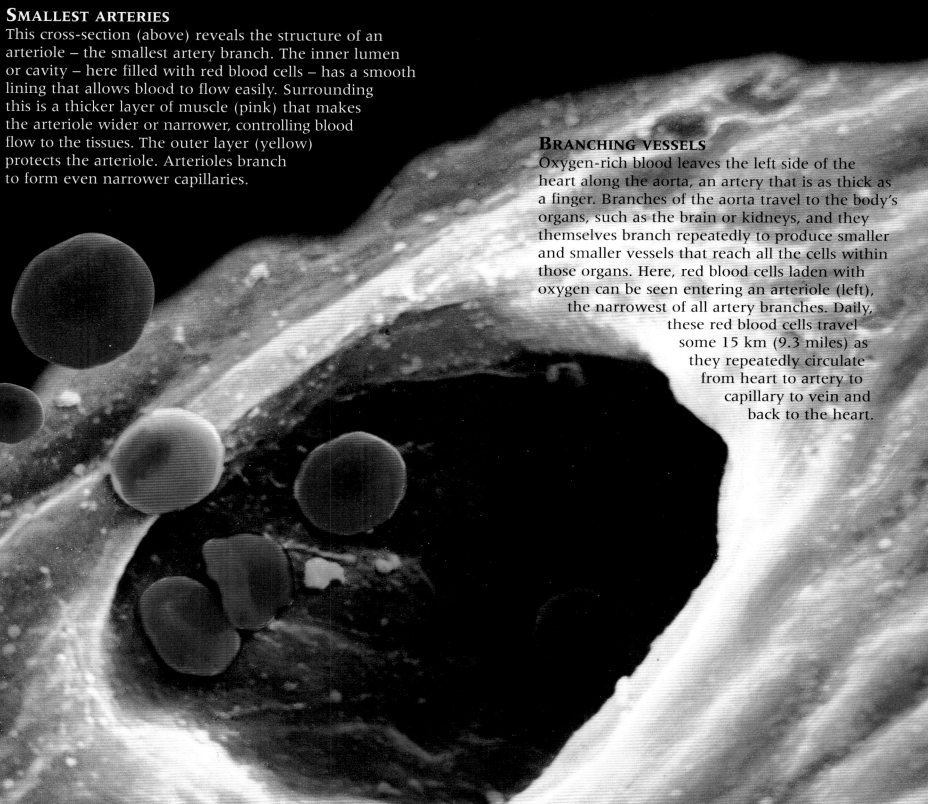

BRANCHING VESSELS

Oxygen-rich blood leaves the left side of the heart along the aorta, an artery that is as thick as a finger. Branches of the aorta travel to the body's organs, such as the brain or kidneys, and they themselves branch repeatedly to produce smaller and smaller vessels that reach all the cells within those organs. Here, red blood cells laden with oxygen can be seen entering an arteriole (left), the narrowest of all artery branches. Daily, these red blood cells travel some 15 km (9.3 miles) as they repeatedly circulate from heart to artery to capillary to vein and back to the heart.

BODY DEFENCES

THE BODY IS UNDER CONSTANT threat from micro-organisms that cause diseases. These pathogens, or germs, include bacteria and viruses. Fortunately, the body has a defence system. First, skin provides a barrier to stop pathogens getting into the blood or tissues. If pathogens do get through, they are attacked by white blood cells called phagocytes and lymphocytes. These are generally found in the bloodstream, and also in the lymphatic system and spleen. Phagocytes hunt down and eat any invaders. Lymphocytes are long-lived cells that make up the body's immune system. They remember specific pathogens and make the body immune or resistant to them by releasing chemicals called antibodies.

TEAR WASH

Each eye has a lacrimal, or tear, gland that releases a constant trickle of watery tears that washes over the eye as the eyelids blink. Sadness or laughter may increase the flow, and the excess tears spill out. Tears wash away dirt and pathogens, and contain a chemical called lysozyme that kills bacteria. Like the skin, tears form part of the body's outer barrier that stops pathogens from entering the body.

PATHOGEN FILTER

As blood passes along capillaries, fluid leaks out to supply cells and return wastes. But excess fluid remains behind and must be returned by the lymphatic system. A one-way network of lymph vessels collects the fluid – lymph – and empties it into two large ducts that return it to the bloodstream. On the way, lymph flows through bean-shaped swellings called lymph nodes where any pathogens are filtered out and destroyed by white blood cells.

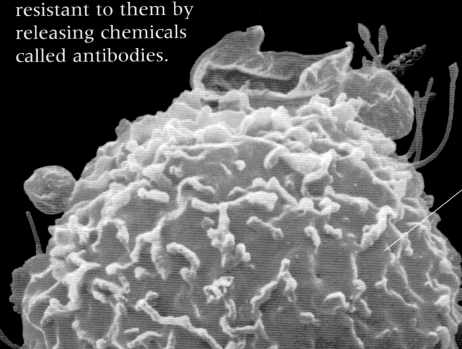

MACROPHAGE
TRAPPING A PATHOGEN

Macrophage tracks down invading pathogens.

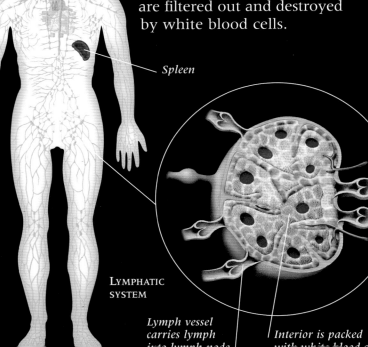

Lymph vessel

Spleen

LYMPHATIC SYSTEM

Lymph vessel carries lymph into lymph node

Interior is packed with white blood cells

BIG EATERS

Equipped with massive appetites, white blood cells called macrophages ("big eaters") roam through tissues, relentlessly hunting invaders. Here a scavenging macrophage has found, engulfed, and is about to digest, the pathogen *Leishmania mexicana*. Spread in the tropics by sandflies, *Leishmania* can cause skin ulcers, fevers, or even death. Macrophages also "present" the remains of dead pathogens to the lymphocytes of the immune system so that they recognize invaders and can launch their own attack

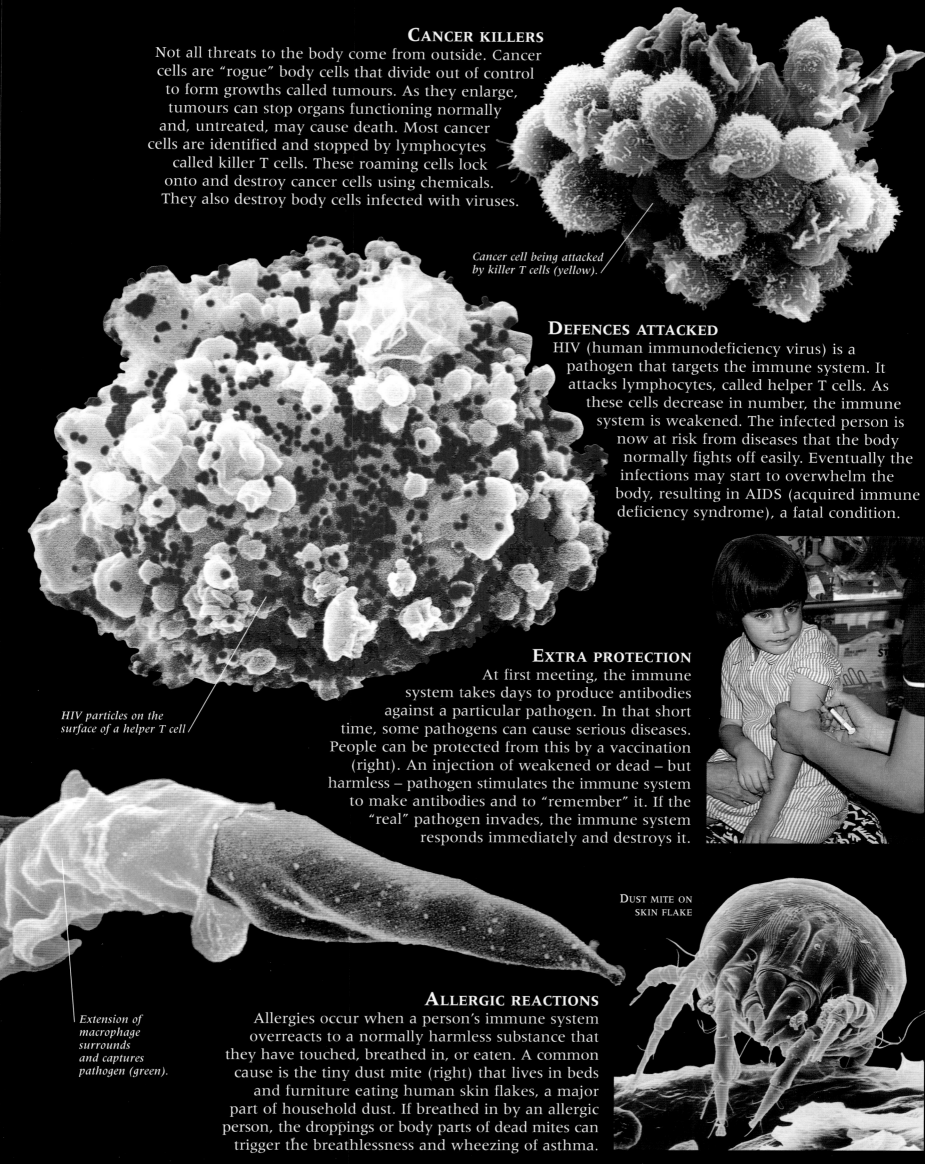

CANCER KILLERS

Not all threats to the body come from outside. Cancer cells are "rogue" body cells that divide out of control to form growths called tumours. As they enlarge, tumours can stop organs functioning normally and, untreated, may cause death. Most cancer cells are identified and stopped by lymphocytes called killer T cells. These roaming cells lock onto and destroy cancer cells using chemicals. They also destroy body cells infected with viruses.

Cancer cell being attacked by killer T cells (yellow).

DEFENCES ATTACKED

HIV (human immunodeficiency virus) is a pathogen that targets the immune system. It attacks lymphocytes, called helper T cells. As these cells decrease in number, the immune system is weakened. The infected person is now at risk from diseases that the body normally fights off easily. Eventually the infections may start to overwhelm the body, resulting in AIDS (acquired immune deficiency syndrome), a fatal condition.

HIV particles on the surface of a helper T cell

EXTRA PROTECTION

At first meeting, the immune system takes days to produce antibodies against a particular pathogen. In that short time, some pathogens can cause serious diseases. People can be protected from this by a vaccination (right). An injection of weakened or dead – but harmless – pathogen stimulates the immune system to make antibodies and to "remember" it. If the "real" pathogen invades, the immune system responds immediately and destroys it.

DUST MITE ON SKIN FLAKE

Extension of macrophage surrounds and captures pathogen (green).

ALLERGIC REACTIONS

Allergies occur when a person's immune system overreacts to a normally harmless substance that they have touched, breathed in, or eaten. A common cause is the tiny dust mite (right) that lives in beds and furniture eating human skin flakes, a major part of household dust. If breathed in by an allergic person, the droppings or body parts of dead mites can trigger the breathlessness and wheezing of asthma.

RESPIRATORY SYSTEM

HUMANS NEED A NON-STOP SUPPLY OF OXYGEN to stay alive. All body cells consume oxygen to obtain energy, but oxygen cannot be stored. And, although air is 21 per cent oxygen, people cannot simply soak it up through their skin. The job of getting oxygen into the body is done by the respiratory system. Its air passages carry air in and out of the lungs, where oxygen gets transferred into the blood and is carried to all cells. Movement of the ribs and diaphragm – called breathing – forces air in and out of the lungs, constantly refreshing supplies. The respiratory system also disposes of carbon dioxide, a waste that would poison the body if it was allowed to build up.

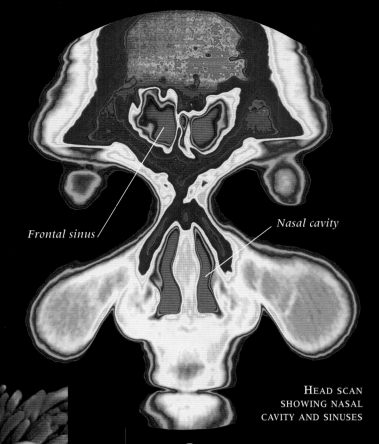

Frontal sinus *Nasal cavity*

HEAD SCAN
SHOWING NASAL
CAVITY AND SINUSES

DUST FILTERS

A carpet of microscopic hair-like cilia line the inside of the nose. They are coated with wet, sticky mucus. As air is breathed in, the mucus captures dust, bacteria, and other particles that would damage the delicate tissues of the lungs. Wave-like beating of the cilia moves the trapped material to the back of the throat where it is swallowed.

CAVITIES AND SINUSES

This scan through the front of the head shows the eye sockets in the centre (black), and the cheek muscles lower left and right (yellow/green). The nasal cavity carries air from the nostrils towards the lungs. The frontal sinuses are part of a network of spaces in the skull connected to the nasal cavity. Sinuses make the skull lighter and, with the nasal cavity, warm and moisten the air being breathed in.

LARYNX

Also called the voice box, because it produces sounds, the larynx connects the throat and the trachea. This inside view (left) shows that the larynx is made of cartilage plates (blue). One of these sticks out at the front, especially in men, as the Adam's apple. The epiglottis folds down during swallowing to stop food getting into the trachea.

Epiglottis

Adam's apple

Vocal cords

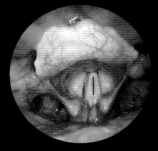

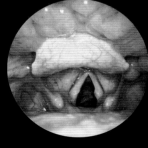

VOCAL CORDS CLOSED   VOCAL CORDS OPEN

POWER PLANTS

Found inside every body cell, these tiny, oval mitochondria (below) are the cell's power plants. They use oxygen to release energy from glucose. This process, called respiration, provides the cell with energy to run its activities. Starved of oxygen – and therefore energy – cells stop working and die. Carbon dioxide, a waste product of respiration, is removed from cells by the bloodstream.

SOUND MAKERS

These views down the throat show the vocal cords stretched across the larynx. During normal breathing, the cords remain open. But if they are closed and air from the lungs is forced through them, the cords vibrate and produce sounds. Tightly stretched cords produce high-pitched sounds, while looser cords make deeper sounds. The lips, teeth, and tongue turn these sounds into recognizable speech.

*Cartilage ring
reinforces trachea.*

*Mitochondria are the
final destination for
breathed-in oxygen.*

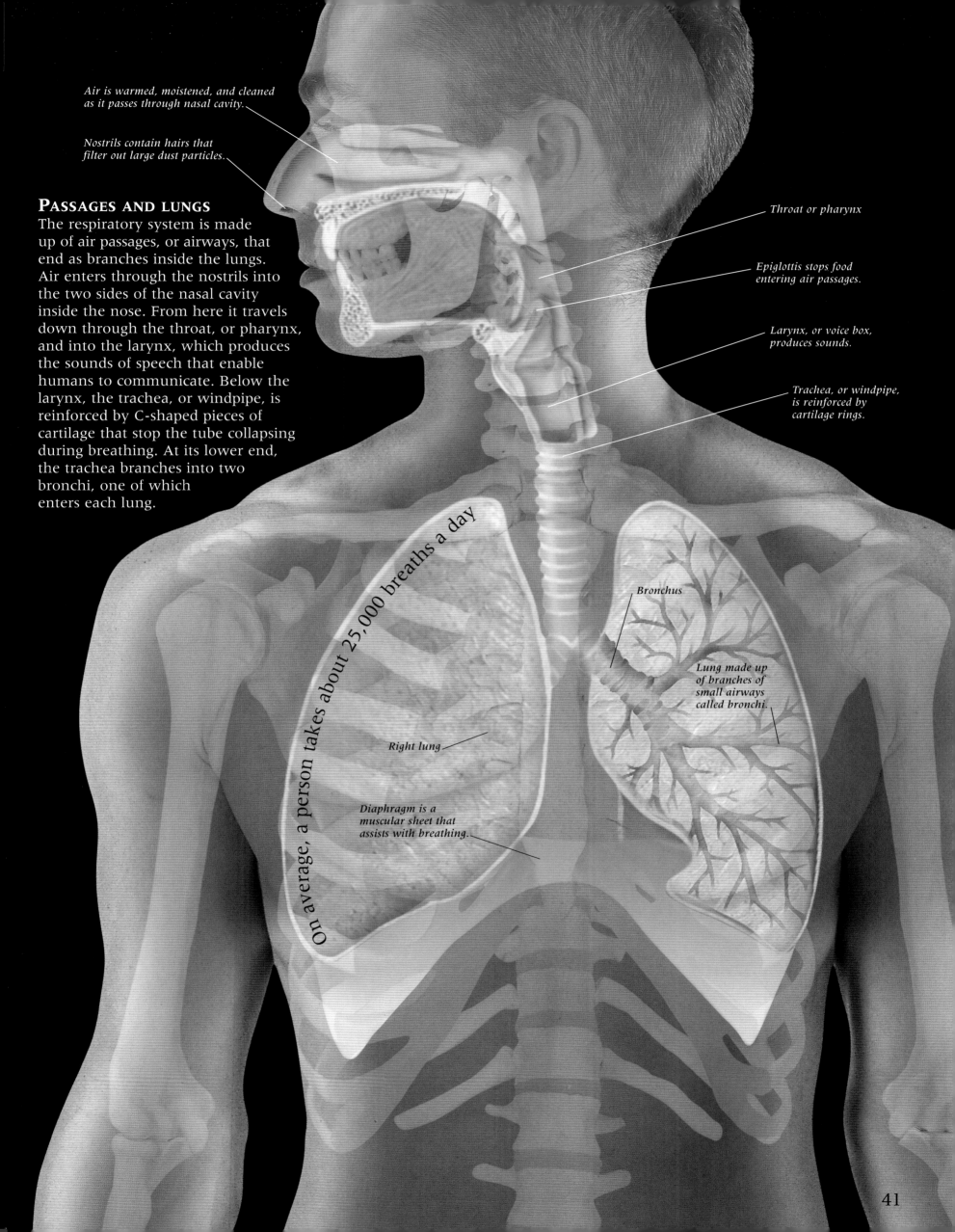

Air is warmed, moistened, and cleaned as it passes through nasal cavity.

Nostrils contain hairs that filter out large dust particles.

Throat or pharynx

Epiglottis stops food entering air passages.

Larynx, or voice box, produces sounds.

Trachea, or windpipe, is reinforced by cartilage rings.

PASSAGES AND LUNGS

The respiratory system is made up of air passages, or airways, that end as branches inside the lungs. Air enters through the nostrils into the two sides of the nasal cavity inside the nose. From here it travels down through the throat, or pharynx, and into the larynx, which produces the sounds of speech that enable humans to communicate. Below the larynx, the trachea, or windpipe, is reinforced by C-shaped pieces of cartilage that stop the tube collapsing during breathing. At its lower end, the trachea branches into two bronchi, one of which enters each lung.

On average, a person takes about 25,000 breaths a day

Bronchus

Lung made up of branches of small airways called bronchi.

Right lung

Diaphragm is a muscular sheet that assists with breathing.

41

LUNGS

INSIDE THE LUNGS, OXYGEN ENTERS – and carbon dioxide leaves – the bloodstream. The cone-shaped lungs take up most of the space inside the thorax. They are surrounded by the ribs, and sit on the diaphragm, a dome-shaped sheet of muscle that separates the thorax from the abdomen below. The lungs feel spongy and light because they consist of a branching network of airways that end in tiny sacs. Together these sacs provide a massive surface through which the maximum amount of oxygen can be transferred into the bloodstream in the shortest time. Breathing constantly refreshes the air inside the lungs, and removes waste carbon dioxide.

BRONCHIAL TREE

The arrangement of airways inside the lungs is often called the bronchial tree because it resembles an upside-down tree. Its "trunk", the trachea, splits into two bronchi – left and right – that carry air in and out of each lung. These bronchi split into smaller bronchi ("branches") and into even smaller bronchioles ("twigs").

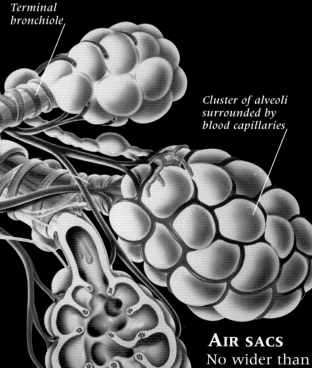

Terminal bronchiole

Cluster of alveoli surrounded by blood capillaries

CAST OF THE AIRWAYS INSIDE THE LUNGS

AIR SACS

No wider than a hair, the tiniest branches of the bronchial tree, called terminal bronchioles, end in clusters of air sacs (bags) called alveoli that look like bunches of grapes. Alveoli are well supplied with the blood capillaries that bring oxygen-poor blood into the lungs to be loaded up with oxygen. There are about 300 million alveoli in the lungs.

GAS EXCHANGE

This microscopic view inside a lung shows air sacs, or alveoli, surrounding a blood capillary carrying red blood cells. The width of the membrane separating blood in the capillary and air inside the alveolus is tiny. Oxygen passes easily from the alveolus into the red blood cells to be taken away. Waste carbon dioxide moves in the opposite direction, to be breathed out.

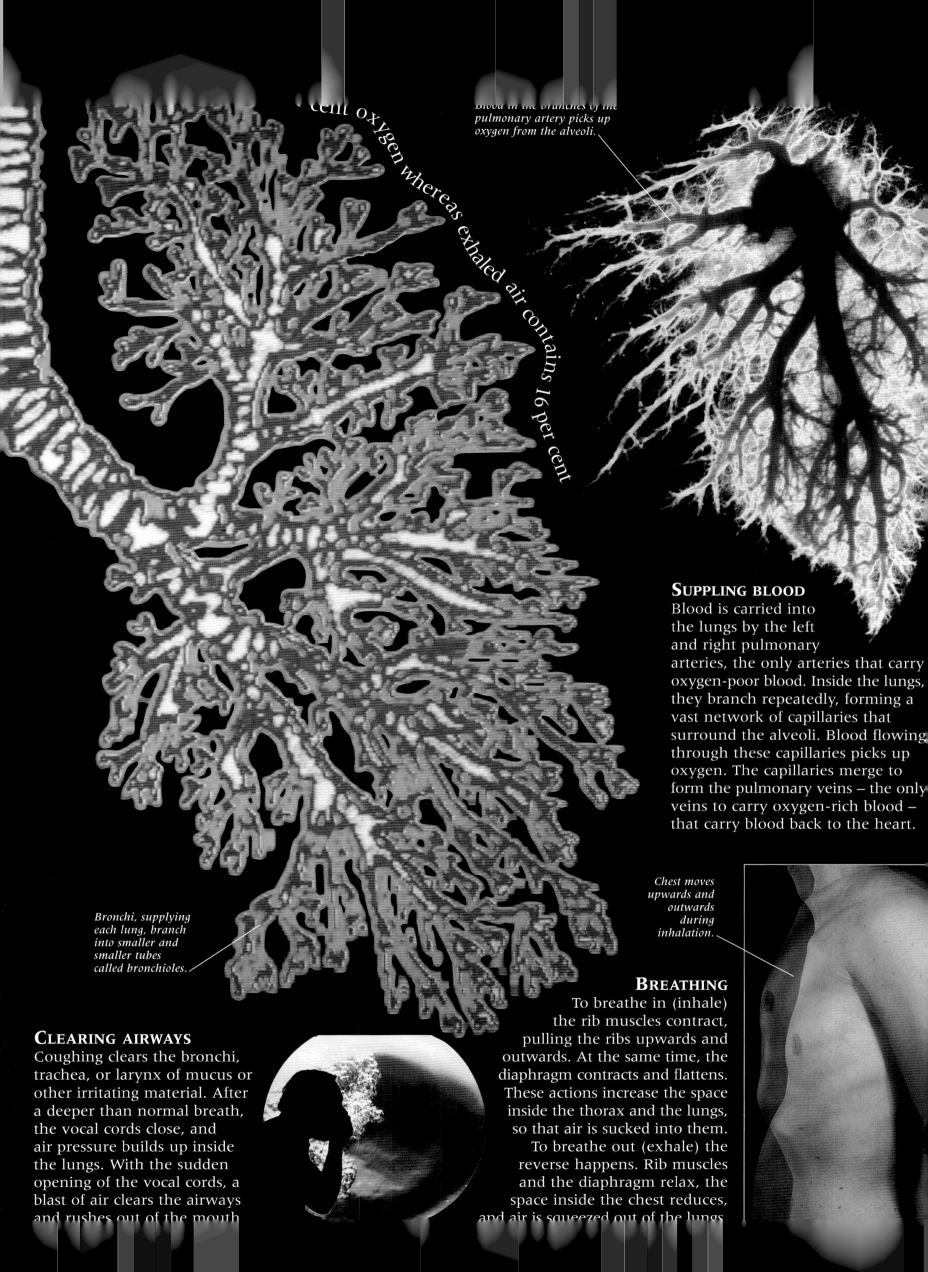

cent oxygen whereas exhaled air contains 16 per cent

Blood in the branches of the pulmonary artery picks up oxygen from the alveoli.

SUPPLING BLOOD

Blood is carried into the lungs by the left and right pulmonary arteries, the only arteries that carry oxygen-poor blood. Inside the lungs, they branch repeatedly, forming a vast network of capillaries that surround the alveoli. Blood flowing through these capillaries picks up oxygen. The capillaries merge to form the pulmonary veins – the only veins to carry oxygen-rich blood – that carry blood back to the heart.

Bronchi, supplying each lung, branch into smaller and smaller tubes called bronchioles.

Chest moves upwards and outwards during inhalation.

BREATHING

To breathe in (inhale) the rib muscles contract, pulling the ribs upwards and outwards. At the same time, the diaphragm contracts and flattens. These actions increase the space inside the thorax and the lungs, so that air is sucked into them. To breathe out (exhale) the reverse happens. Rib muscles and the diaphragm relax, the space inside the chest reduces, and air is squeezed out of the lungs

CLEARING AIRWAYS

Coughing clears the bronchi, trachea, or larynx of mucus or other irritating material. After a deeper than normal breath, the vocal cords close, and air pressure builds up inside the lungs. With the sudden opening of the vocal cords, a blast of air clears the airways and rushes out of the mouth

TEETH AND MOUTH

THE MOUTH IS THE ENTRANCE to the digestive system. Its front teeth, firmly anchored in the jaw bones, grip food and pull it into the mouth, aided by the lips. Salivary glands then deliver a stream of watery saliva to the mouth. Powerful jaw muscles pull the lower jaw upwards with great force enabling the cheek teeth to crush the saliva-soaked food into a pulp. Cheek muscles contract to keep the food between the teeth, while the muscular tongue mixes food with saliva and tastes it. Once well-chewed, the ball, or bolus, of food, glistening with slippery saliva, is pushed by the tongue towards the throat, ready for swallowing.

Pink gums cover the jaw bone and surround the tooth like a tight collar.

Enamel

Dentine

Pulp cavity

SECTION THROUGH A MOLAR TOOTH

Root canal

Root

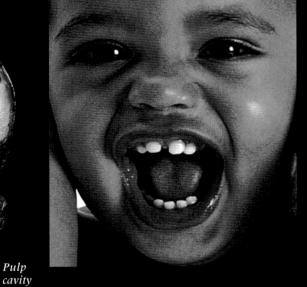

FIRST SET

A young child shows off her teeth, the first of two sets she will have during her lifetime. These milk, or deciduous ("falling off"), teeth first appear at six months of age. By about two years of age, there are 20 in all. Between the ages of six and 12, her milk teeth are gradually pushed out by a second set of permanent teeth.

INSIDE A TOOTH

Covering the crown of this molar tooth (left) is a layer of hard-wearing, protective enamel. Beneath the enamel, bone-like dentine, which extends down into the molar's twin roots, gives the tooth its shape. The central pulp cavity contains blood vessels and nerve fibres that enter the tooth through thin root canals to feed the tooth and give it sensation.

The crown – the white part above the gum – of this incisor is shaped for cutting food.

DENTINE

Dentine, which makes up the bulk of the tooth, is very similar to bone but is much harder. Under the microscope, dentine can be seen to have a network of tiny channels (right). These carry fibres from nerve endings that make dentine very sensitive to temperature extremes and touch, both of which are felt as pain.

TOOTH TYPES

By the late teens, most people have a full set of 32 permanent teeth, 16 in each jaw, upper and lower. This full complement includes four types of teeth. Eight chisel-like incisors and four pointed canines bite and tear food. Behind them, eight flat-topped pre-molars crush food into a pulp, a job completed with great force by the 12 larger molars at the back of the jaws.

Every day...
a person's salivary glands release more than 1 litre (0.22 gallons) of saliva.

Some cells inside this salivary gland release mucus, others water and enzymes.

Tooth enamel is the hardest substance in the body

Tooth enamel contains no cells so, if it is damaged by decay, it can only be replaced with a filling.

TOOTH DECAY
This molar (left) has tooth decay. The white enamel has been eaten away to expose the dentine underneath. Tooth decay is caused by plaque, a mixture of food and bacteria that builds up if teeth are not brushed regularly. Bacteria feed on sugars in food, releasing acids that eat away at enamel, exposing the inside of the tooth and causing pain called toothache.

SALIVA PRODUCERS
This is a view inside one of the six glands that make and release saliva into the mouth. Saliva moistens food, cleans the mouth, and dissolves chemicals in food so it can be tasted. It also includes enzymes that digest starch, and slippery mucus that sticks food together, making swallowing easier.

The back molars – wisdom teeth – sometimes do not appear, or cause pain and have to be removed

The canines, or eye-teeth, pierce and grip food as it is pulled into the mouth.

DIGESTION

FOOD IS AN ESSENTIAL part of life. It provides the body with energy, as well as the raw materials for growth and repair. However, most foods are mixtures of large, complex molecules that cannot be used by the body until processed by the digestive system. After being eaten, food is digested, or broken down, into small, simple molecules, such as glucose or amino acids. Digestion is achieved by crushing and mashing food, and by the use of enzymes – chemicals that increase the speed by which food is broken down. Digested food is then absorbed into the bloodstream. Finally, any undigested food is removed from the body.

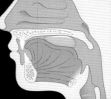

| STAGE ONE | STAGE TWO |

SWALLOWING

The act of swallowing moves food from mouth to stomach. In the first stage, the tongue pushes chewed food (brown) to the back of the throat. In the second stage, food touches the throat and triggers a reflex reaction. A wave of muscle contractions carries food into the oesophagus.

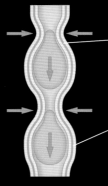

Muscles contract here to push food forward.

Muscles relax here to allow food to slide forward easily.

PUSHING FORCE

Food is pushed along the oesophagus, and other parts of the alimentary canal, by a process called peristalsis. Inside the oesophagus wall a layer of circular muscle contracts behind each bolus (ball) of food, and propels it towards the stomach.

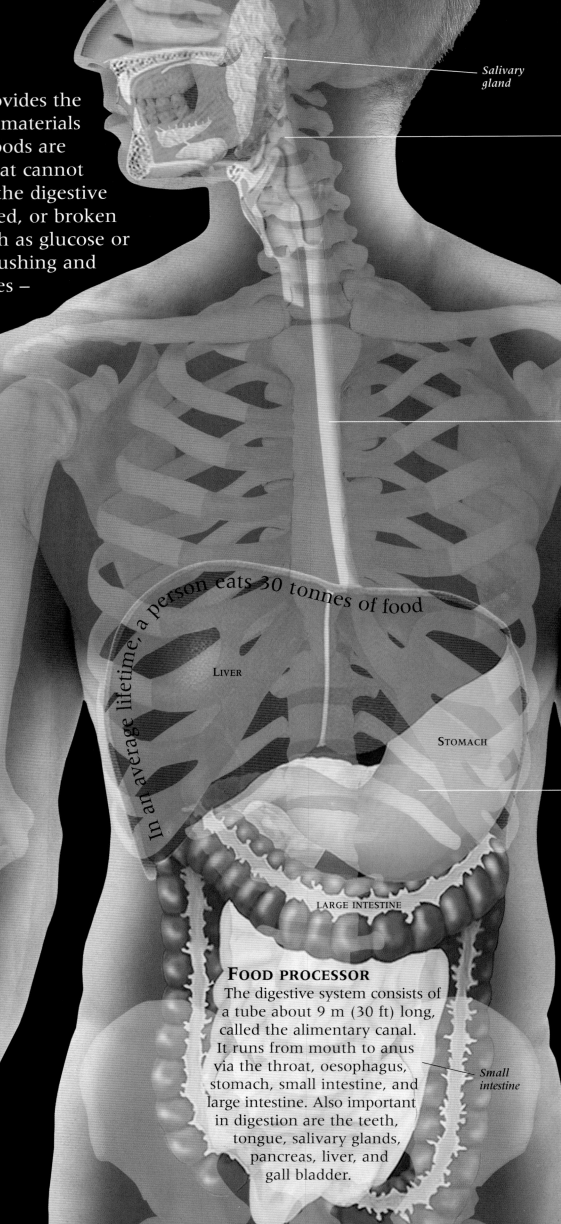

Salivary gland

In an average lifetime, a person eats 30 tonnes of food

LIVER

STOMACH

LARGE INTESTINE

FOOD PROCESSOR

The digestive system consists of a tube about 9 m (30 ft) long, called the alimentary canal. It runs from mouth to anus via the throat, oesophagus, stomach, small intestine, and large intestine. Also important in digestion are the teeth, tongue, salivary glands, pancreas, liver, and gall bladder.

Small intestine

INTO THE THROAT

This photo shows the view (left) that food would have just before it was swallowed. It also shows the muscular tongue, which pushes chewed food towards the throat, or pharynx, at the back of the mouth. Dangling in the middle is the uvula, part of the soft palate that moves upwards during swallowing to stop food going into the nose. The bulges on either side are the tonsils, part of the lymphatic system, that help to destroy bacteria taken in with food.

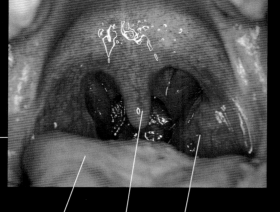

Tongue Uvula Tonsil

OESOPHAGUS

The oesophagus, or gullet, does not have any role in digesting food. This 25-cm (10-in)-long tube does, however, have the vital job of carrying food from the throat to the stomach. Lubricated with slimy mucus, food is pushed down the oesophagus by waves of muscular contraction called peristalsis. The journey from mouth to stomach takes about 10 seconds.

Cells lining the oesophagus have a folded surface that traps mucus and makes the food slip down smoothly.

STOMACH SECRETIONS

When food reaches the stomach, it is churned and mashed by contractions of muscles in the stomach wall. It is also mixed with gastric juice released from deep inside these gastric (stomach) pits (right). Here, glands release juice containing strong hydrochloric acid and an enzyme called pepsin. Cells (blue) in the stomach's lining release mucus. This covers the lining and stops the powerful gastric juice from digesting the stomach wall.

MODEL OF A
PEPSIN MOLECULE

This indented "active site" of the enzyme is where proteins are attached before being split into smaller molecules.

CHEMICAL DIGESTERS

Pepsin (left) is an enzyme – chemical digester – contained in the gastric juice that is secreted into the stomach when food arrives. It works rapidly, in the very acidic environment provided by the hydrochloric acid in gastric juice, to break down proteins into smaller molecules called peptides. The hydrochloric acid in gastric juice also destroys bacteria swallowed with food or drinks.

INTESTINES

WHEN FOOD LEAVES THE STOMACH, it moves into the small, and then large, intestine. The small intestine has three parts. First, there is the short duodenum that receives chyme – part-digested food – from the stomach, bile from the liver, and digestive juices from the pancreas. Here and in the next part, the jejunum, food is digested by enzymes. In the third and longest section, the ileum, food is absorbed into the bloodstream. Undigested food then passes into the colon, the longest part of the large intestine, where water is absorbed into the bloodstream. The remaining dried-out waste, together with dead cells and bacteria, forms faeces, which are stored in the rectum and pushed out during defecation.

After swallowing, it takes 10 seconds for food to reach the stomach.

MONDAY 12 NOON
When food reaches the stomach, it looks chopped up after being chewed.

Pyloric sphincter (start of small intestine)

MONDAY 3 PM
Two to four hours later, food leaves the stomach and passes into the small intestine, looking like a thick soup.

Enzymes in the duodenum break down fats, carbohydrates, and proteins.

FLOW CONTROL
Rings of muscle (sphincters) control the flow of food as it passes through the digestive system. When food has been churned into creamy chyme by the muscular stomach walls, the pyloric sphincter, at the exit of the stomach, relaxes and opens, squirting chyme into the duodenum.

Pyloric sphincter controls food flow from stomach.

Food spends between three and six hours in the small intestine

SMALL INTESTINE
This X-ray (above) shows the coils of a healthy small intestine (green) filling much of the space inside the abdomen, and extending from the stomach (blue, top right) to where it joins the large intestine (bottom, left). The small intestine gets its name from the fact that at 2.5 cm (1 in) wide, it is much narrower than the 6.5-cm (2.5-in)-wide large intestine.

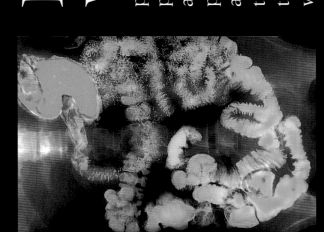

FOOD ABSORBERS
A forest of minute, finger-like villi covers the inside of the small intestine, giving it a velvety texture. As liquid food swirls past, enzymes on the surface of villi complete the digestion of food into simple nutrients. These are absorbed rapidly by the numerous villi, and are carried away by the blood that flows through them.

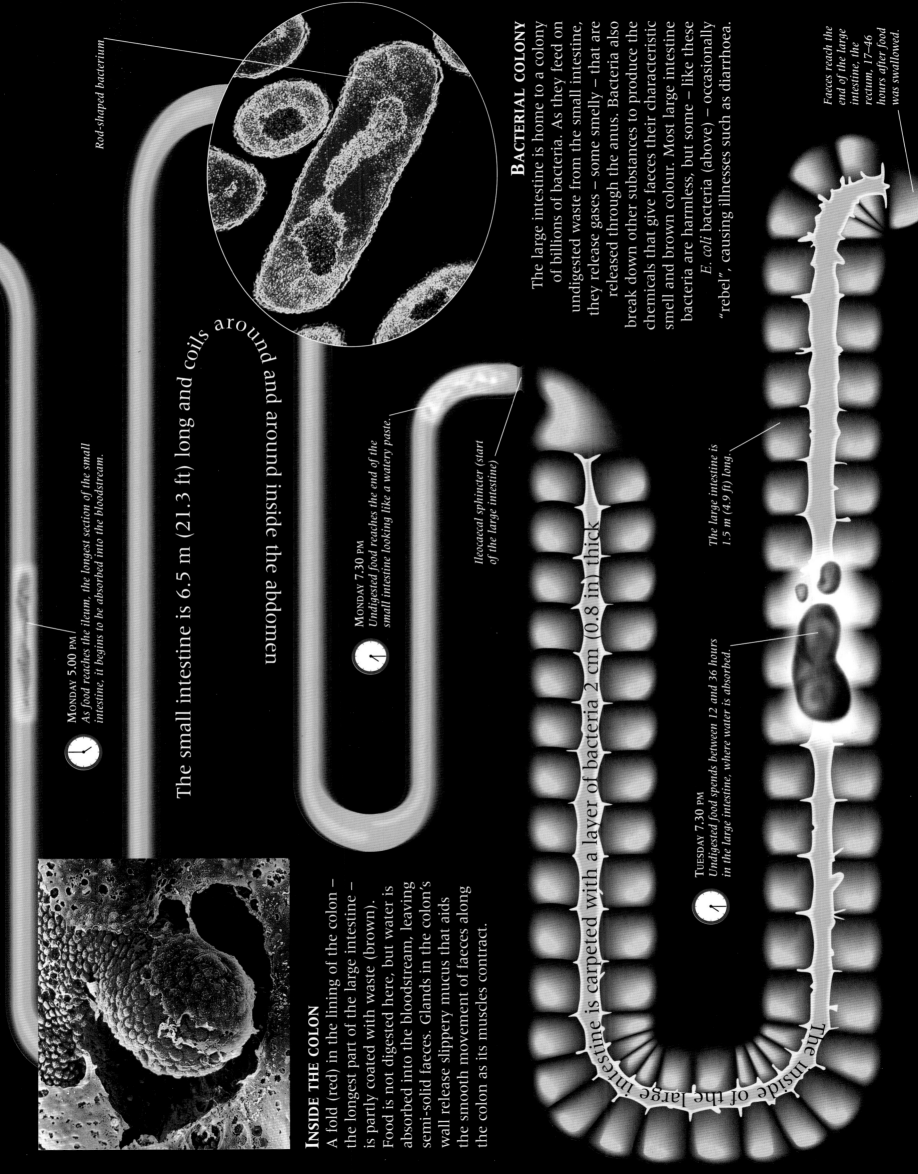

Rod-shaped bacterium

The small intestine is 6.5 m (21.3 ft) long and coils around and around inside the abdomen

MONDAY 5.00 PM
As food reaches the ileum, the longest section of the small intestine, it begins to be absorbed into the bloodstream.

MONDAY 7.30 PM
Undigested food reaches the end of the small intestine looking like a watery paste.

Ileocaecal sphincter (start of the large intestine)

INSIDE THE COLON
A fold (red) in the lining of the colon – the longest part of the large intestine – is partly coated with waste (brown). Food is not digested here, but water is absorbed into the bloodstream, leaving semi-solid faeces. Glands in the colon's wall release slippery mucus that aids the smooth movement of faeces along the colon as its muscles contract.

BACTERIAL COLONY
The large intestine is home to a colony of billions of bacteria. As they feed on undigested waste from the small intestine, they release gases – some smelly – that are released through the anus. Bacteria also break down other substances to produce the chemicals that give faeces their characteristic smell and brown colour. Most large intestine bacteria are harmless, but some – like these *E. coli* bacteria (above) – occasionally "rebel", causing illnesses such as diarrhoea.

Faeces reach the end of the large intestine, the rectum, 17–46 hours after food was swallowed.

The large intestine is carpeted with a layer of bacteria 2 cm (0.8 in) thick

The large intestine is 1.5 m (4.9 ft) long.

TUESDAY 7.30 PM
Undigested food spends between 12 and 36 hours in the large intestine, where water is absorbed.

The inside of the large intestine

LIVER

MOST OF THE SPACE IN THE upper right abdomen is taken up by the liver, the body's chemical factory and largest internal organ. The liver carries out more than 500 functions. Its millions of cells constantly process blood to make sure it has the correct chemical composition. Many of its functions are linked to digestion. Food-rich blood is received straight from the small intestine where it has been absorbed. The liver then adjusts the food content before blood is generally circulated. This is done by storing or releasing glucose and fats, and by chemically treating amino acids (which make up proteins). The liver also stores vitamins and iron, and produces a liquid called bile, that helps digest fats. Other liver functions include breaking down poisons, and the disposing of hormones produced by the body once they have done their job.

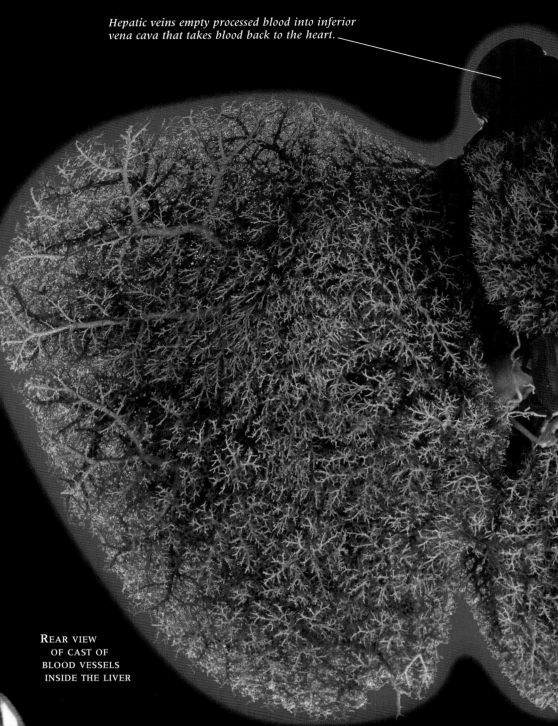

Hepatic veins empty processed blood into inferior vena cava that takes blood back to the heart.

REAR VIEW
OF CAST OF
BLOOD VESSELS
INSIDE THE LIVER

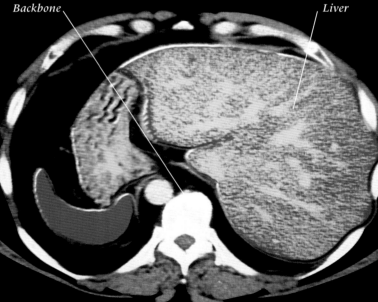

Backbone *Liver*

LIVER BLOOD VESSELS
This cast reveals the massive network of blood vessels that carries blood to and from liver cells. The hepatic portal vein (pale blue) brings blood laden with food from the small intestine, while oxygen-rich blood from the heart is delivered by the hepatic artery (centre red). The two blood supplies mix in channels called sinusoids. Blood leaving the liver empties into the inferior vena cava, the large vein that returns blood from the lower body to the heart.

BODY SLICE
The large size of the liver can be seen clearly in this CT scan (above) which shows a "slice" through the upper abdomen. Next to the liver are the stomach (green) and the spleen (pink). The spleen is part of the lymphatic system that contains white blood cells that fight disease, and which filters worn-out blood cells from the bloodstream.

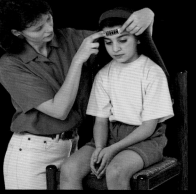

HEAT GENERATOR
The thousands of chemical reactions that take place inside the liver generate heat that warms blood as it passes through. This helps the body maintain a constant high internal temperature of about 37°C (98.6°F), which can be measured using a temperature strip like this. Temperatures that are too high or low may indicate illness.

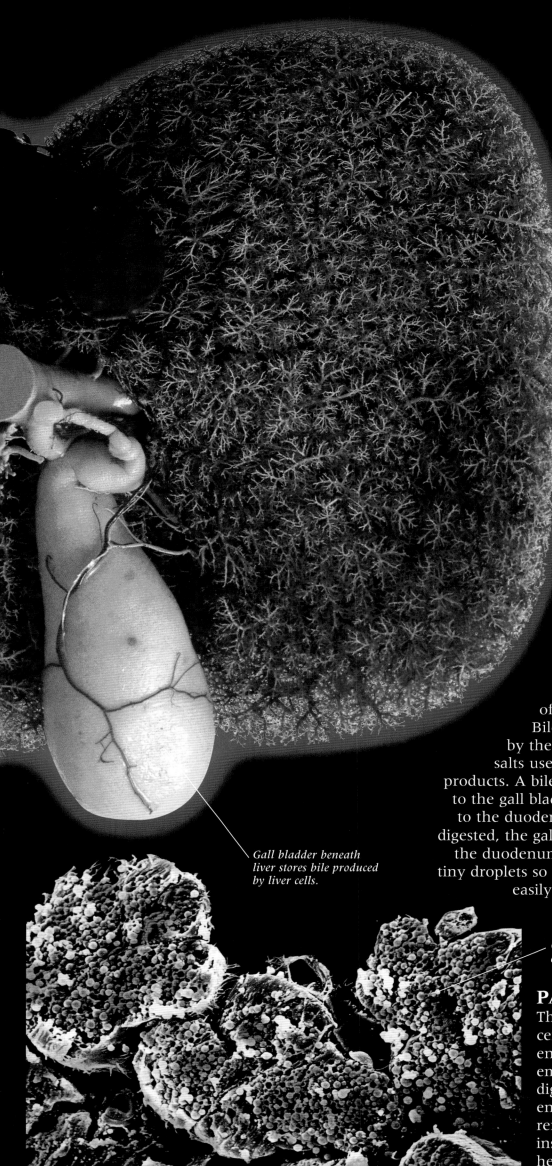

Gall bladder beneath liver stores bile produced by liver cells.

Red blood cells passing along sinusoid

LIVER CELLS

Inside the liver, millions of liver cells, or hepatocytes (brown), are arranged in regular patterns around blood channels called sinusoids (blue). These carry food-rich blood directly from the small intestin and oxygen-rich blood from the heart. As blood flows along the sinusoid, hepatocyt take in, and release, substances. They also release bile along tiny bile capillaries (green). Other cells remove debris, worn-out cells, and pathogens. After blood has passed through the liver, it has been thoroughly processed and cleaned.

BILE STORE

The gall bladder is a muscular bag at the rear of the liver that stores bile. Bile, a greenish liquid made by the liver, is a mixture of bile salts used in digestion, and waste products. A bile duct (tube) delivers bile to the gall bladder, and also connects it to the duodenum. When food is being digested, the gall bladder squirts bile into the duodenum. Bile salts turn fats into tiny droplets so that they can be digested easily and rapidly by enzymes.

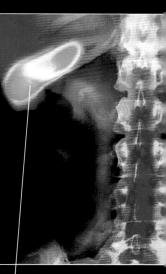

X-ray shows gall bladder at one side of the backbone.

Globules inside these pancreas cells contain digestive enzymes.

PANCREAS

The pancreas has two distinct jobs. Firstly, 99 per cent of its cells make digestive enzymes. These enzymes are released into the pancreatic duct that empties them into the duodenum, where they help digest food. This photo (left) shows the cells with enzyme-containing globules inside. Secondly, the remaining 1 per cent of cells release the hormones insulin and glucagon into the bloodstream. These help to control glucose levels in the blood.

URINARY SYSTEM

AS BLOOD CIRCULATES AROUND the body, it is continually checked and cleaned by the two kidneys. First, the kidneys remove excess water from the blood so its volume is always the same. This also ensures that the body's water content – about 52 per cent in young women and 60 per cent in young men – remains constant. Second, the kidneys extract wastes, particularly urea, that would be harmful if allowed to build up in the blood. The resulting mix of 95 per cent water plus dissolved waste is called urine. This is flushed out of the body through the ureters, bladder, and urethra which, with the kidneys, make up the urinary system. The importance of the kidneys is shown by the fact that every four minutes the body's total blood volume passes through them.

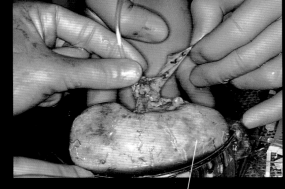

Ureter carries urine away from kidney.

X-RAY OF THE ABDOMEN SHOWING THE URINARY SYSTEM

KIDNEY TRANSPLANT

Sometimes kidneys stop working properly, either through injury or disease, and poisonous wastes build up in the bloodstream. If this happens, doctors can take a healthy kidney – either from a living donor (giver) or someone who has just died – and attach it to the blood supply of the person with defective kidneys. This operation is called a kidney transplant. Just one transplanted kidney enables the body to operate normally.

Healthy kidney prepared for transplant

Bladder receives urine and stores it until it is released down the urethra out of the body.

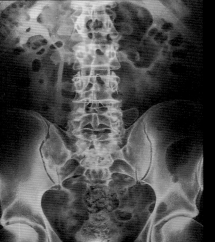

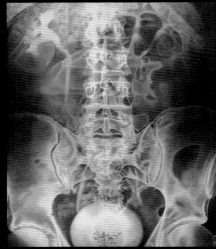

EMPTY BLADDER   FULL BLADDER

WASTE DISPOSAL

As these X-rays (above) show, the bladder (green) expands greatly to store urine. As it fills, stretch sensors in the bladder wall send nerve signals to the brain, and the person feels the need to urinate. The exit from the bladder is closed by a sphincter, or ring of muscle. When a person goes to the toilet, they relax the sphincter, and urine flows out of the bladder along the urethra, squeezed out by the bladder's muscular wall.

Kidneys filter 180 litres (48 gallons) of fluid from blood daily... 1.5 litres (0.4 gallons) becomes urine, the rest returns to the blood

Pelvis of the right kidney

INSIDE THE KIDNEY

Each bean-shaped, 12 cm- (4.7 in-) long kidney has three main sections, as this CT scan (right) shows. The outer cortex (blue/yellow) surrounds the medulla with its cone-shaped sections called pyramids (orange/ yellow). Inside the medulla is the hollow pelvis (red). The renal artery brings blood into the kidney. Its many branches carry blood to one million tiny filtering units called nephrons. These are long tubules that loop from cortex to medulla to cortex before emptying into the pelvis. They process liquid filtered from the blood to produce urine.

Pelvis

Renal artery

CROSS-SECTION OF A KIDNEY

Pyramids in kidney's medulla

Blood capillaries, which make up a glomerulus, filter liquid out of blood to be processed.

KIDNEY GLOMERULUS

MOVING URINE

After urine has been made in the outer part of each kidney, it flows into the inner, hollow region called the pelvis. From here a narrow tube about 30 cm (12 in) long – the ureter – travels down the abdomen to enter the back of the bladder. Waves of muscular contractions, called peristalsis, pass down the wall of each ureter, pushing a constant trickle of urine into the bladder. Periodically, urine is released from the bladder through the urethra.

FILTRATION UNIT

Each nephron, or filtering unit, of a kidney has a tight ball of blood capillaries called a glomerulus (above) and a thin tube called the renal tubule. High blood pressure forces liquid out of blood flowing through the glomerulus, filtering it through capillary walls into the renal tubule. As liquid flows along the tubule, useful substances, such as glucose and water, are returned to the bloodstream. Excess water and waste form urine.

REPRODUCTION

Humans are no different from any other living thing in their need to produce offspring to replace them when they die. Babies are made by sexual reproduction. This involves the joining together of special sex cells, made by the reproductive system – the only body system that differs between males and females. The main parts of the female system are the two ovaries, the uterus, and the vagina. When a girl is born, her ovaries contain a lifetime supply of sex cells called eggs, or ova. In the male system, two testes make sex cells called sperm – short for spermatozoa – that are released through the penis. A sperm is about 50 times narrower than an egg. Both reproductive systems only start working at puberty, generally when a girl or boy is in their early teens. A woman's ovaries release one egg each month as part of a regular cycle. A man's testes produce millions of sperm daily throughout his lifetime.

FEMALE REPRODUCTIVE SYSTEM

The two ovaries produce and release eggs. These are carried along the fallopian tubes to the thick-walled, muscular uterus, inside which the baby develops during pregnancy. The uterus opens to the outside through the vagina, which is also how sperm enter a woman's reproductive system.

Ovary

Fallopian tube

Uterus   Vagina

MALE REPRODUCTIVE SYSTEM

Two egg-shaped testes produce sperm. They are connected by sperm ducts (tubes) to the urethra, the tube that carries both urine and sperm outside the body through the penis. Sperm production needs cooler temperatures than normal. For that reason, the testes hang outside the body.

Prostate gland

Penis

Testis

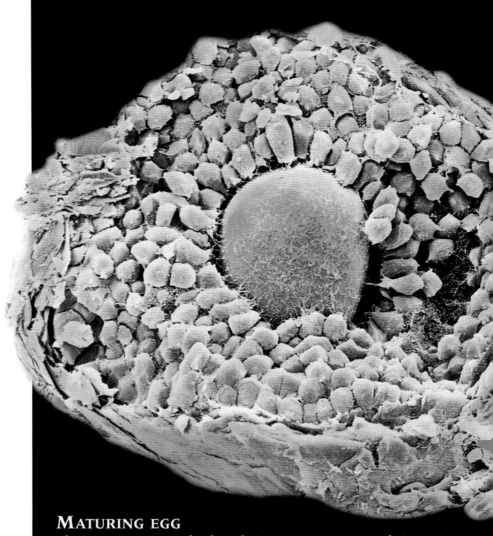

MATURING EGG

The ovaries are packed with immature eggs, each in a tiny "bag" called a follicle (above). Every month, a few follicles start to enlarge. The egg (pink) inside matures, while the surrounding follicle cells (blue) protect and nourish it, and produce a fluid. Eventually, one fluid-filled follicle outgrows the others, ruptures, and releases its ripe egg.

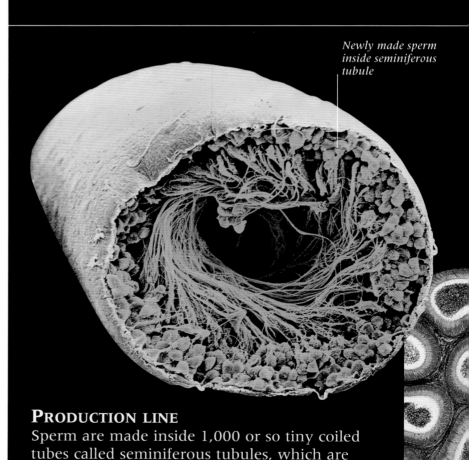

Newly made sperm inside seminiferous tubule

PRODUCTION LINE

Sperm are made inside 1,000 or so tiny coiled tubes called seminiferous tubules, which are packed inside each testis. This view inside a tubule (above) shows a swirl of sperm (blue) being made and fed by cells in the tubule's lining. Every day, the two testes produce more than 300 million sperm.

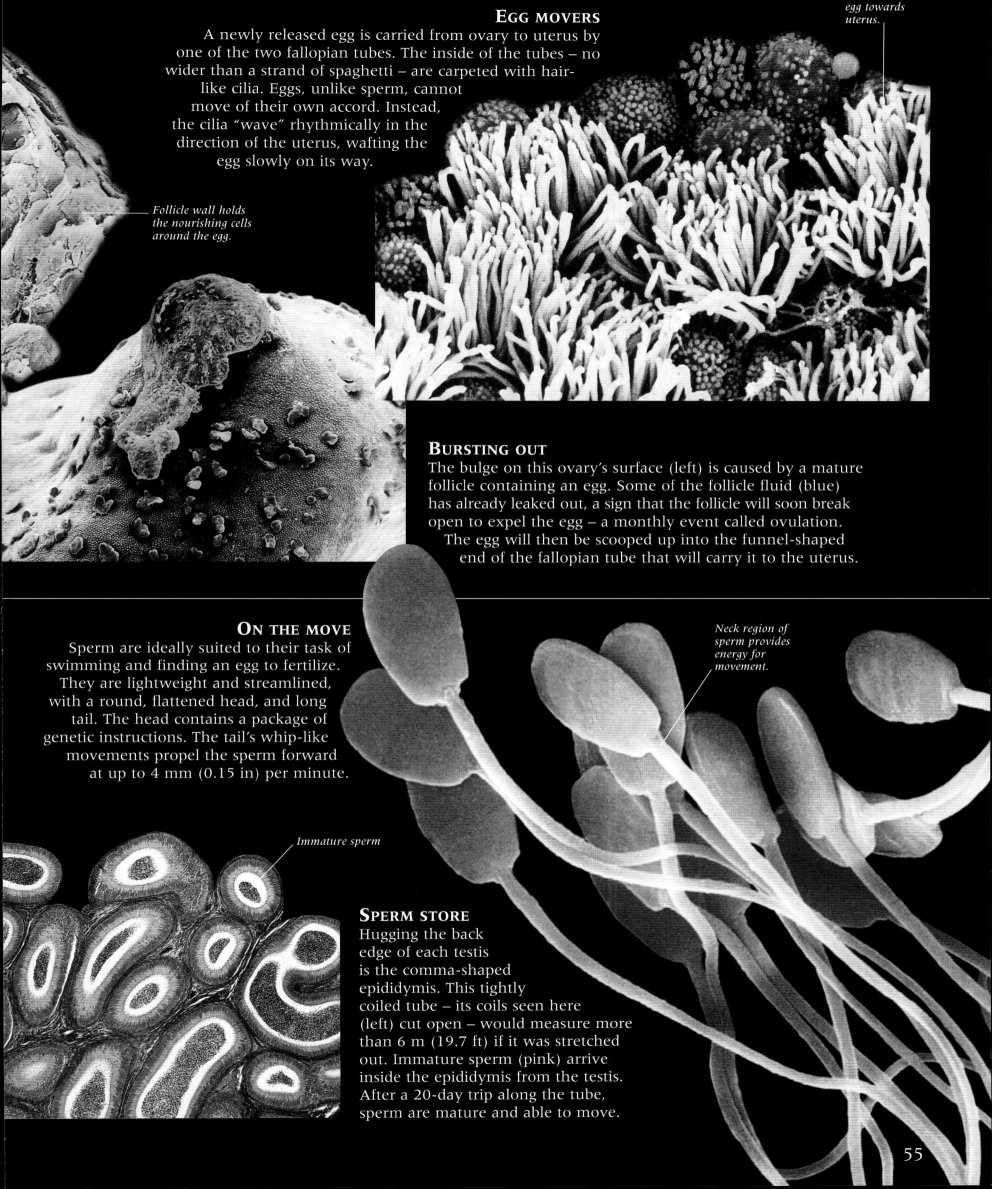

EGG MOVERS

A newly released egg is carried from ovary to uterus by one of the two fallopian tubes. The inside of the tubes – no wider than a strand of spaghetti – are carpeted with hair-like cilia. Eggs, unlike sperm, cannot move of their own accord. Instead, the cilia "wave" rhythmically in the direction of the uterus, wafting the egg slowly on its way.

egg towards uterus.

Follicle wall holds the nourishing cells around the egg.

BURSTING OUT

The bulge on this ovary's surface (left) is caused by a mature follicle containing an egg. Some of the follicle fluid (blue) has already leaked out, a sign that the follicle will soon break open to expel the egg – a monthly event called ovulation. The egg will then be scooped up into the funnel-shaped end of the fallopian tube that will carry it to the uterus.

ON THE MOVE

Sperm are ideally suited to their task of swimming and finding an egg to fertilize. They are lightweight and streamlined, with a round, flattened head, and long tail. The head contains a package of genetic instructions. The tail's whip-like movements propel the sperm forward at up to 4 mm (0.15 in) per minute.

Neck region of sperm provides energy for movement.

Immature sperm

SPERM STORE

Hugging the back edge of each testis is the comma-shaped epididymis. This tightly coiled tube – its coils seen here (left) cut open – would measure more than 6 m (19.7 ft) if it was stretched out. Immature sperm (pink) arrive inside the epididymis from the testis. After a 20-day trip along the tube, sperm are mature and able to move.

FERTILIZATION AND PREGNANCY

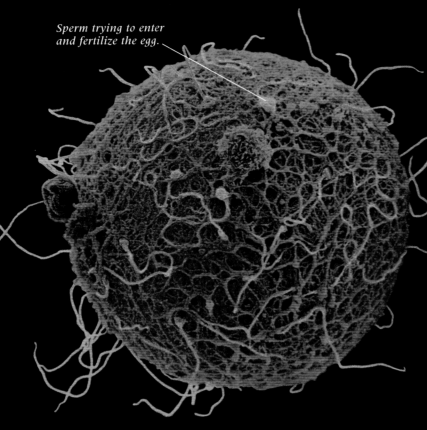

*Sperm trying to enter
and fertilize the egg.*

BIRTH MARKS THE END of pregnancy, a period
that began some 38 weeks earlier when
the baby's parents had sexual intercourse.
During this intimate and personal act, a man
releases hundreds of millions of sperm
inside his partner by putting his penis in
her vagina. The sperm swim through
her uterus towards the fallopian tubes,
although only a few hundred reach their
destination. If these survivors meet with
an egg that has just been released from
an ovary, one sperm will join with, and
fertilize, that egg. Fertilization brings together
the genetic material from mother and father,
producing the instructions needed to make
a new human being. After a week travelling
along the fallopian tube, the fertilized egg
attaches itself to the lining of the uterus
where it develops into a baby.

COMPETING SPERM
Tails lashing, hundreds of sperm (green) surround an
egg (red), each trying to get through the coat around it.
Eventually, a single sperm breaks through, losing its
tail in the process. Immediately, chemical changes
inside the egg block the entry of any other sperm.
The sperm's nucleus combines with the egg's nucleus.
This is the moment that the egg becomes fertilized.

HOLLOW BALL
Five days after fertilization the egg has reached the
end of the fallopian tube and divided several times,
to become a hollow ball of cells – a blastocyst. As it
arrives in the uterus, the blastocyst sheds the coat
(below) that originally surrounded the egg when
it left the ovary. A day later, the blastocyst burrows
into the soft wall of the uterus. Here, its outer cells
form part of the placenta – the
organ that links the
blood supply of
mother and baby.
The inner cells
develop into
an embryo.

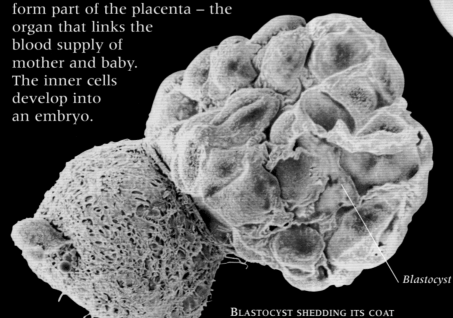

Blastocyst

BLASTOCYST SHEDDING ITS COAT

*Developing
eye*

*Umbilical cord
connects the
embryo to the
placenta in the
mother's uterus.*

FIRST WEEKS
Four weeks after fertilization, repeated divisions have
turned the fertilized egg into an apple pip-sized embryo
made of millions of cells. These cells are forming organs
such as the liver and lungs. The heart is already beating
and the network of blood vessels is spreading. A simple
brain is in place, and the rest of the nervous system is
developing. On the outside, the first signs of arms and
legs – called limb buds – can be seen.

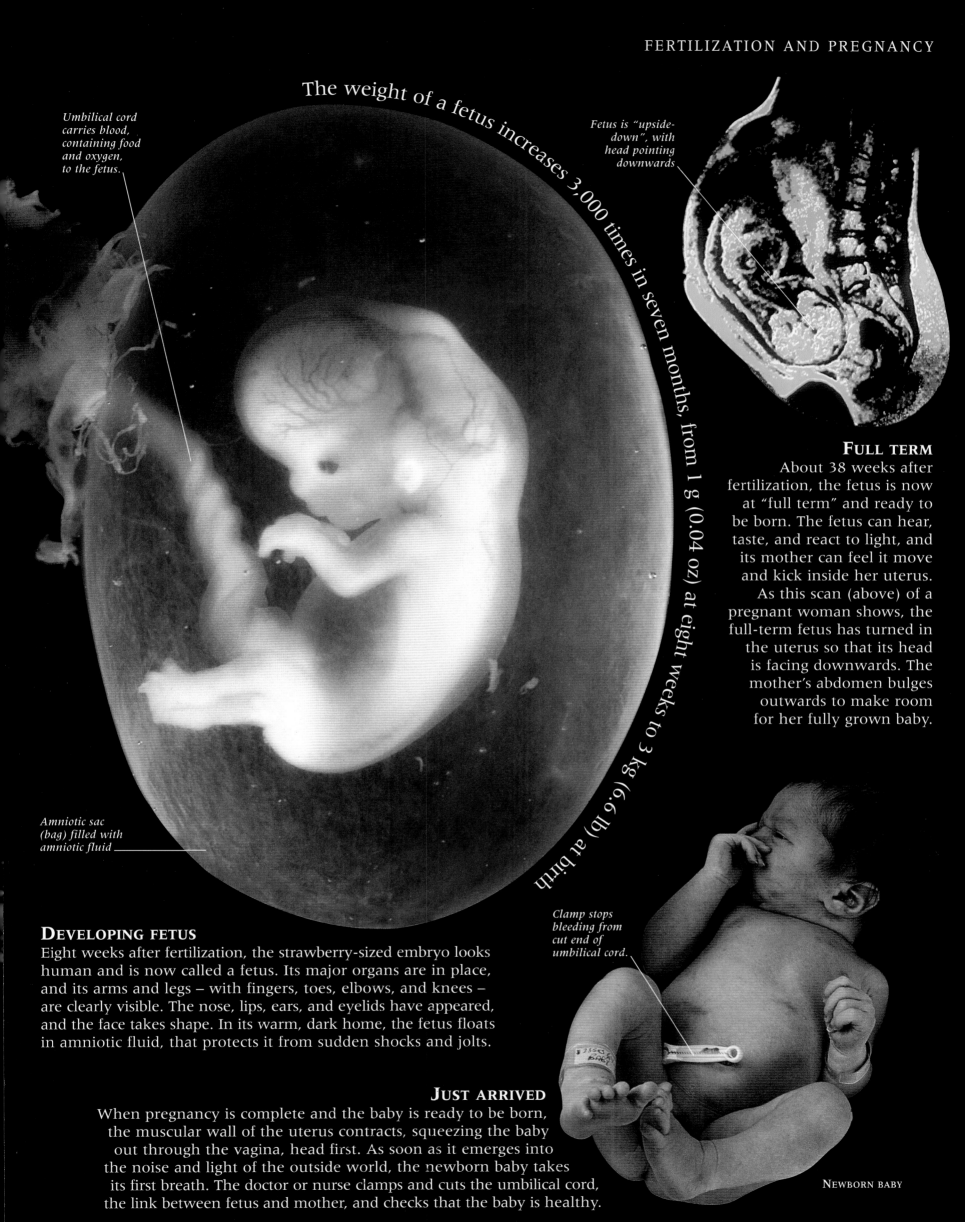

Umbilical cord carries blood, containing food and oxygen, to the fetus.

The weight of a fetus increases 3,000 times in seven months, from 1 g (0.04 oz) at eight weeks to 3 kg (6.6 lb) at birth

Fetus is "upside-down", with head pointing downwards

FULL TERM

About 38 weeks after fertilization, the fetus is now at "full term" and ready to be born. The fetus can hear, taste, and react to light, and its mother can feel it move and kick inside her uterus. As this scan (above) of a pregnant woman shows, the full-term fetus has turned in the uterus so that its head is facing downwards. The mother's abdomen bulges outwards to make room for her fully grown baby.

Amniotic sac (bag) filled with amniotic fluid

DEVELOPING FETUS

Eight weeks after fertilization, the strawberry-sized embryo looks human and is now called a fetus. Its major organs are in place, and its arms and legs – with fingers, toes, elbows, and knees – are clearly visible. The nose, lips, ears, and eyelids have appeared, and the face takes shape. In its warm, dark home, the fetus floats in amniotic fluid, that protects it from sudden shocks and jolts.

Clamp stops bleeding from cut end of umbilical cord.

JUST ARRIVED

When pregnancy is complete and the baby is ready to be born, the muscular wall of the uterus contracts, squeezing the baby out through the vagina, head first. As soon as it emerges into the noise and light of the outside world, the newborn baby takes its first breath. The doctor or nurse clamps and cuts the umbilical cord, the link between fetus and mother, and checks that the baby is healthy.

NEWBORN BABY

GENES AND CHROMOSOMES

INSIDE THE NUCLEUS OF EVERY BODY CELL is a set of instructions that controls not only what is happening inside that cell, but also what the body looks like and does. This "library" of instructions takes the form of molecules called DNA. Its "books" are short sections of DNA called genes. Each gene contains a coded message controlling a particular feature. A cell's DNA is packed into convenient "sections" – 23 pairs of chromosomes. Within each pair, one chromosome is from a person's mother and one from their father. Each pair shares the same array of genes, but may carry slightly different versions of them, some of which are inactive. If, for example, a person inherits a gene for blue eyes from one parent, but brown eyes from the other, only the "brown" gene is active, and the person has brown eyes.

DNA PACKAGES

Each chromosome contains part of a cell's DNA. When a cell divides, the DNA become tightly coiled and the chromosomes appear like this (left), with two identical arms. These form when the DNA inside makes exact copies of itself. When the cell divides, the chromosomes split so that each daughter cell receives identical instructions.

Chromosome consists of two identical arms, or chromatids, joined in the middle.

"Backbone" of one of the strands in this DNA molecule

MODEL OF
DNA MOLECULE

More than 100,000 genes are found on the 46 chromosomes in the nucleus of every body cell.

IDENTIFYING GENES

In the 1990s the Human Genome Project started to identify and locate all the genes contained in the 46 human chromosomes. Here, a technician prepares small sections of chromosome to work out the precise chemical structure of the DNA in its genes. By 2000, the project was complete.

Head of second twin

Head of first twin

TWINS

Ultrasound scans provide a safe way to view a fetus developing inside its mother's uterus. In this scan, twin fetuses can be seen. Identical twins are produced if a fertilized egg splits into two separate cells. They share exactly the same genes, and must be the same sex. Fraternal twins, produced when two eggs are fertilized, do not share identical genes, so need not be the same sex.

PASSING ON GENES

A child receives genes from both parents because, during fertilization, the sperm and egg's chromosomes mix. The two sets of chromosomes may contain different versions of the same genes. The new combination means that a child may share features, such as eye colour, with one or both parents, but will also have their own unique features.

Chromosome pair number 20

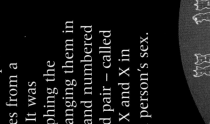
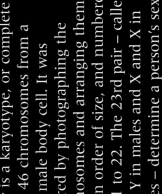

MOLECULE OF LIFE

DNA – or deoxyribonucleic acid – is the cell's information store. Each DNA molecule consists of two long strands that are wrapped around each other to form a structure called a double helix. The "backbone" of each strand is made up of sugar and phosphate molecules (light blue). Projecting inwards are bases (spheres) that are paired with bases on the opposite strand, like rungs of a ladder. The precise sequence of base pairs in one section of DNA – a gene – provides just one of the instructions needed to build and run a cell.

Link between base pairs on opposite strands on DNA

each human cell contains three million base pairs

Chromosome pair number 9

Eight base pairs are shown on this stretch of DNA...

X and Y sex chromosomes

COMPLETE SET

Below is a karyotype, or complete set, of 46 chromosomes from a single male body cell. It was prepared by photographing the chromosomes and arranging them in pairs in order of size, and numbered from 1 to 22. The 23rd pair – called X and Y in males and X and X in females – determine a person's sex.

GROWTH AND AGEING

D URING A LIFETIME, THE HUMAN BODY follows a predictable pattern of growth in the early years and ageing in the later years. Growth happens rapidly in the first year or so, proceeds steadily throughout childhood, accelerates again during the early teen years, and then comes to a halt. As the body grows in childhood, the head becomes smaller in proportion to the rest of the body, the arms and legs become comparatively longer, and the face changes shape. Between nine and 14, the process of adolescence begins. This changes children into adults. The way boys and girls think and feel alters. A period of change, called puberty, starts their reproductive systems working and produces adult features, such as breasts in girls and facial hair in boys. Growth ceases in the late teens and adulthood begins. In later life, as body cells become less efficient, the ageing process takes over, and features such as wrinkling skin and greying hair appear.

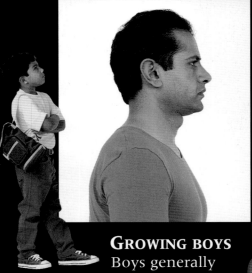

GROWING GIRLS
For girls, puberty often begins between nine and 13, and lasts for about three years. Girls grow suddenly, and are taller than boys of the same age for a while. Their breasts develop, their hips widen, and their body shape changes to that of a woman. Their reproductive system "switches on" and they have periods and ovulate – releasing an egg each month.

GROWING BOYS
Boys generally start puberty between the ages of 10 and 14. They have a sudden growth spurt, and hair grows on their face, bodies, armpits, and around the genitals. As his reproductive system starts to work, the boy's testes make sperm. The larynx (voice box) gets larger – and may be noticeable as the Adam's apple (above) – making the voice "break" and go deeper. The body becomes more muscular with broader shoulders.

DEVELOPING BONES
As a baby develops inside its mother, its skeleton forms from flexible cartilage. Gradually, the cartilage is replaced by bone, in a process called ossification ("bone making"), which continues until the late teens. In the X-rays below, bone (blue/white) shows up, but cartilage does not. The hands of the infant and child show "gaps", because parts of the bones are still made of cartilage. By 13 years old, ossification has occurred widely. However, cartilage is still being replaced, notably near the ends of the long palm and finger bones. In the 20-year-old's hand, bone growth is complete.

Finger bone growing in length

Wrist "bones" not visible as they are still made of cartilage.

HAND X-RAY OF
1 YEAR OLD (LEFT) AND
3 YEAR OLD (RIGHT)

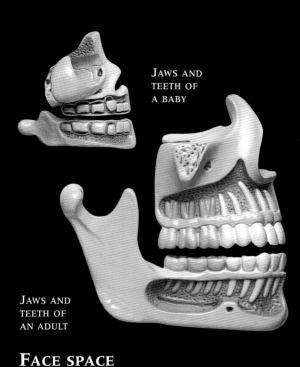

JAWS AND
TEETH OF
A BABY

JAWS AND
TEETH OF
AN ADULT

BLOCKED ARTERIES

One result of ageing is the buildup of fatty deposits inside arteries which may cause a blood clot, or thrombus, to form. This coronary artery (right), which supplies blood to the muscular wall of the heart, has a thrombus (red) blocking about 30 per cent of its width. If the thrombus interrupts the blood supply, the heart muscle becomes starved of oxygen and causes a heart attack.

FACE SPACE

When a baby is born, its jaw bones are small compared to the rest of the skull, and its first set of teeth – milk teeth – still lie beneath the gums. During childhood, the jaws increase greatly in size so that the face "grows out" of the skull and changes in shape and appearance. A second, bigger, set of permanent teeth replaces the milk teeth and fills the enlarged jaws.

BRITTLE BONES

With age, bones become less dense, more brittle, and more likely to break. This condition, called osteoporosis, is more serious in women than in men. This X-ray of a person with osteoporosis shows the vertebrae (orange) as wedge-shaped because they have been crushed by the downward weight of the body.

Vertebra is squashed by body's weight.

Growth in this band of cartilage between the head and shaft makes bone grow longer.

By the age of 20, the bones in the hand are fully grown.

HAND X-RAY OF
13 YEAR OLD (LEFT) AND
20 YEAR OLD (RIGHT)

BODY DATA

MAJOR MEDICAL DISCOVERIES

c.420BC Greek physician Hippocrates taught the importance of observation and diagnosis – rather than magic and myth – in medicine.

c.190 Influential Greek doctor, Galen, described – often incorrectly – the way the body worked and his ideas remained until the 1500's.

c.128 Arab physician Ibn An-Nafis showed that blood flows through the lungs.

1543 First accurate description of human anatomy published by Belgian anatomist Andreas Vesalius.

1628 British doctor William Harvey described how blood circulates around the body, pumped by the heart.

1663 Blood capillaries observed by Italian physiologist Marcello Malpighi.

1674 Antonie van Leeuwenhoek from Holland observed and described sperm using an early microscope.

1691 British doctor Clopton Havers described the structure of bone.

1796 First vaccination – against smallpox – by British doctor Edward Jenner.

1811 British anatomist Charles Bell showed that nerves were made of bundles of neurons (nerve cells).

1816 Stethoscope invented by French doctor René Laënnec.

1846 Ether first used as an anaesthetic in surgery by US dentist William Morton.

1851 German physicist Hermann Helmholtz invented the ophthalmoscope, an instrument for looking inside the eye.

1860s French scientist Louis Pasteur explained how micro-organisms cause infectious diseases.

1865 Joseph Lister, a British doctor, first used antiseptic during surgery to reduce deaths from infection.

1882 Bacterium that causes TB (tuberculosis) identified by German doctor Robert Koch.

1895 X-rays discovered by German physicist Wilhelm Roentgen.

1900 Blood groups A, B, AB, and O, discovered by Austrian-born US doctor, paving the way for safe blood transfusions.

1903 ECG (electrocardiograph), a device for monitoring heart activity, invented by Dutch physiologist Willem Einthoven.

1906 British biochemist Frederick Gowland Hopkins shows the importance of vitamins in food.

1910 German scientist Paul Ehrlich discovered Salvarsan, the first drug used to treat a specific disease.

1921 Canadians Frederick Banting and Charles Best isolated the hormone insulin, allowing diabetes to be controlled.

1928 British doctor Alexander Fleming discovered penicillin, the first antibiotic.

1933 Electron microscope invented by German electrical engineer Ernst Ruska.

1943 Dutch doctor Willem Kolff invents the kidney dialysis machine to treat people with kidney failure.

1953 Using research by British physicist Rosalind Franklin, USA biologist James Watson and British physicist Francis Crick discovered the structure of DNA.

1953 US surgeon John Gibbon first used the heart-lung machine he invented to pump, and add oxygen to, blood during heart surgery.

1954 Polio vaccine, developed by US physician Jonas Salk, first used.

1954 Successful kidney transplant carried out in Boston, USA.

1958 Ultrasound first used to check health of a foetus in its mother's uterus by British professor Ian Donald.

1967 South African surgeon Christiaan Barnard carried out first successful heart transplant.

1972 CT (computerized tomography) scanning first used to produce images of organs.

1978 Successful IVF (in vitro fertilization) by British doctors Patrick Steptoe and Robert Edwards results in first "test tube" baby, Louise Brown.

1979 Vaccination finally eradicates smallpox.

1980 Introduction of "keyhole" surgery – using an endoscope to look inside the body through small incisions.

1981 AIDS (acquired immune deficiency syndrome) identified as a new disease.

1982 First artificial heart, invented by US scientist Robert Jarvik, implanted into a patient.

1983 French scientist Luc Montagnier discovers the HIV virus that causes AIDS.

1986 Human Genome Project launched to analyse the DNA in human chromosomes.

1999 Chromosome 22 became first human chromosome to have DNA sequenced.

2000 First "draft" of Human Genome Project completed.

BODY FACTS

- Our eyes are closed for half an hour a day due to blinking.
- One third of living bone is water.
- The femur (thigh bone) is one quarter of our height.
- The heart beats 100,800 times a day.
- At any moment, 75 per cent of blood is in veins, 20 per cent in arteries, and 5 per cent in capillaries.
- The human body has 10–100 trillion bacterial cells, either on it or in it.
- No two people share the same fingerprints, not even identical twins.
- The lungs contain a network of airways 2,400 km (1,491 miles) long.
- In total, a person's nerves extend more than 150,000 km (93,210 miles).
- A typical adult brain weighs about 1.3 kg (3 lb).
- The brain loses about 1,000 cells each day which are never replaced.
- On average, there are 100,000 hair follicles on the human head and 80 hairs are lost from it each day.
- Humans use 200 different muscles to walk.
- A person is about 1 cm (0.4 in) taller in the morning than in the evening, because cartilage in the spine becomes compressed during the day.
- Eggs, produced by the ovaries, are the biggest human body cells.
- A baby's head is one quarter of its body length, but by adulthood it is only one eighth.

KILLER T CELLS ATTACKING CANCER CELLS

BRANCHES OF MEDICINE

Name	What it deals with
Cardiology	Heart and arteries
Dermatology	Skin
Endocrinology	Hormones
Epidemiology	Causes and spread of diseases
Gastroenterology	Stomach, intestines
Geriatrics	Elderly people
Gynaecology	Female reproductive organs
Haematology	Blood
Immunology	Immune system
Neurology	Brain and nerves
Ophthalmology	Eyes
Obstetrics	Pregnancy and birth
Oncology	Tumours and cancers
Orthopaedics	Bones, joints, and muscles
Paediatrics	Children
Pathology	Effects of diseases
Psychiatry	Mental illness
Radiology	Imaging techniques

GLOSSARY OF BODY TERMS

Abdomen lower part of the trunk – central part of the body – between the chest and the legs

Absorption taking in digested food from the small intestine to the bloodstream

Adolescence a period of time during the teenage years when the body changes from that of a child to an adult

Allergy illness caused by over-reaction of the body's immune system to a normally harmless substance, such as pollen

Alveoli microscopic air bags inside the lungs through which oxygen enters the bloodstream

Angiogram special X-ray that shows blood vessels

Antibody substance released by immune (defence) system that marks pathogens for destruction

Atrium one of the two upper chambers – left and right – of the heart

Blood vessel tube that carries blood through the body. The main types are arteries, veins, and capillaries

Cartilage tough, flexible material that forms parts of structures, such as the nose and larynx (voice box), and covers the ends of bones

Cells tiny living units that are the basic building blocks of the body

Cerebrum the largest part of the brain which enables people to think, and feel, and makes the body move

Chromosome one of 46 information packages that contains DNA inside every cell

Cilia hair-like projections from certain cells

CT scan special type of X-ray that produces images that "slice" through the body

Diaphragm sheet of muscle that separates the chest from the abdomen, and plays an important part in breathing

Digestion breakdown of food by the digestive system into simple nutrients that the body can use

DNA (deoxyribonucleic acid) chemical that contains the instructions to build and operate a cell, and that is found inside a chromosome

Embryo baby in the early stages of development, up to eight weeks after fertilization

Enzyme chemical that greatly speeds up the breakdown of food during digestion

Faeces solid waste remaining after digestion, that is expelled through the anus

Fertilization joining together of egg and sperm during reproduction

Fetus the name given to a developing baby from eight weeks after fertilization until birth

Gland group of cells that release chemicals into or onto the body

Hepatic to do with the liver

Hormone chemical messenger produced by an endocrine gland and carried in the blood

Joint part of the skeleton where two or more bones meet

Keratin tough, waterproof protein found in hair, nails, and the outer layer of skin

Ligament tough straps that hold bones together at joints

Melanin brown pigment that colours skin and hair

Mitochondria tiny structures inside cells that release energy from food

MRI scan uses magnetism and radio waves to produce images of the inside of the body

Mucus thick, slippery fluid that lines the respiratory and digestive systems

Muscle tissue that can contract and cause movement

Nephrons tiny units inside the kidneys that filter blood and produce urine

Neurons nerve cells that make up the brain, spinal cord, and nerves, and carry electrical signals at high speed

Nucleus control centre of a cell. Contains chromosomes

Nutrient substances in food that are useful to the body

Organ major body part, such as the heart or brain, made up of different tissues, with a specific role or roles

Pathogens disease-causing microscopic organisms such as bacteria or viruses

Peristalsis waves of muscle contraction that push food through the digestive system

Puberty period during early teenage years when reproductive systems start working

Reflex automatic action such as swallowing, blinking, or pulling a hand away from a sharp object

Renal to do with the kidney

Respiration release of energy from food inside cells

Sweat salty, waste liquid released onto the skin that helps to cool the body

System group of linked organs that work together to do a particular job

Thorax upper part of the trunk – central part of the body – also called the chest, between the neck and the abdomen

Tendon tough cord or sheet that links muscle to bone

Thermogram image that shows the amount of heat given out by different body regions

Tissue collection of similar cells that have one particular role

Ultrasound scan image produced by beaming sound waves into the body

Urine waste liquid produced inside the kidneys

Ventricle one of the two (left and right) lower chambers of the heart

X-rays invisible rays used to produce images of hard parts of the body, such as bone

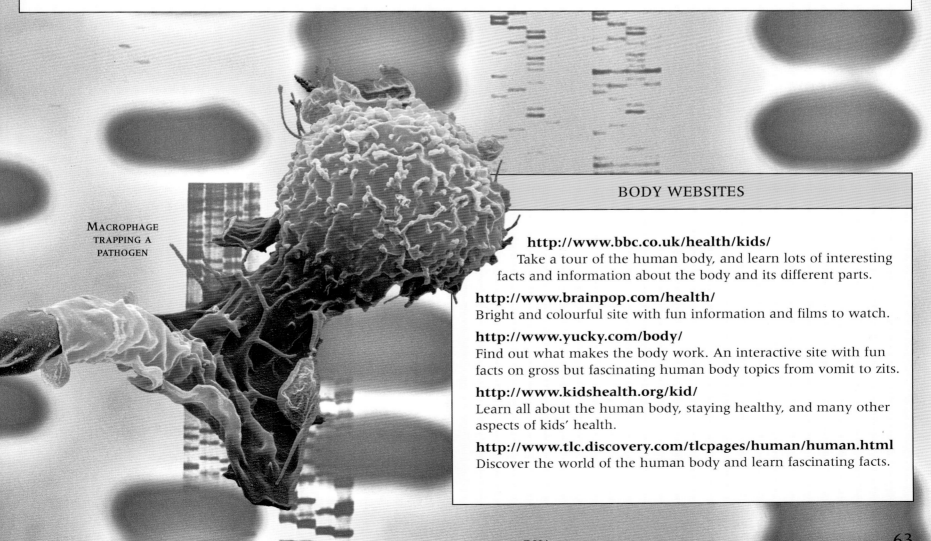

MACROPHAGE TRAPPING A PATHOGEN

BODY WEBSITES

http://www.bbc.co.uk/health/kids/
Take a tour of the human body, and learn lots of interesting facts and information about the body and its different parts.

http://www.brainpop.com/health/
Bright and colourful site with fun information and films to watch.

http://www.yucky.com/body/
Find out what makes the body work. An interactive site with fun facts on gross but fascinating human body topics from vomit to zits.

http://www.kidshealth.org/kid/
Learn all about the human body, staying healthy, and many other aspects of kids' health.

http://www.tlc.discovery.com/tlcpages/human/human.html
Discover the world of the human body and learn fascinating facts.

INDEX

CREDITS

Dorling Kindersley would like to thank: Joanna Pocock for design help; Lynn Bresler for proofreading and the index; Gary Ombler for special photography; Diane Legrande for DK picture research; Mark Gleed for modelling; and John Bell & Croyden for supplying the skeleton.
Addition photography: Geoff Brightling, Geoff Dann, Philip Dowell, Jo Foord, Steve Gorton, Alistair Hughes, Dave King, Ray Moller, Susanna Price, Dave Rudkin, Colin Salmon, Mike Saunders.
The author would like to thank: Kitty, Jo, Lucy, Fran, Marcus, and Robin for the hard work, creative insights, and attention to detail that have made this book possible. Author's photograph by Tony Nandi.

Dorling Kindersley would also like to thank the following for their kind permission to reproduce their photographs:

a = above, b = below, c = centre, l = left, r = right, t = top

3B Scientific: 54bl; **Art Directors & TRIP:** H. Rogers 39cr; **Corbis UK Ltd:** Galen Rowell 34t; Olivier Prevosto 7tl; **Denoyer-Geppert Int:** 2bc, 18bl, 36bl; **Educational and Scientific Products Limited:** 8b; **gettyone stone:** 59tl; Paul Dance 38tl; Ron Boardman 18–19; Spike Walker 44cl; **Robert Harding Picture Library:** 19cr; CNRI/ Phototake NYC 1, 8-9; Michael Agliolo/Int'l Stock 44-45; Phototake 56tl; R. Francis 27br; **Image Bank:** 59tr; **National Medical Slide Bank:**

22c; **Oxford Scientific Films:** G. W. Willis 45cr; **Royal College of Surgeons:** 50-51; **Science Photo Library:** 8c, 9cr, 28cl, 29cr, 43tr; Adam Hart-Davis 15bc; Alfred Pasieka 5tr, 19tl, 42-43, 50cl, 53tr, 58-59, 61ca, 62-63; Andrew Syred 3ca, 3c, 3br, 6cl, 7tr, 11c, 30-31; Astrid & Hanns-Frieder Michler 15cra, 25c, 54-55b; Biophoto Associates 2tl, 10-11, 43br, 49tc, 58b, 59bc, 59l; Brad Nelson/ Custom Medical Stock Photo 52c; BSIP 48bl; BSIP VEM 27cb, 32bc, 40ca; Catherine Pouedras 10bl; CNRI 4cl, 11br, 36cl, 37tr, 42bc, 44bc, 52-53, 54br; D. Phillips 55br; Daudier, Jerrican 2-3, 16b; David Parker 20tr, 20-21; David Scharf 7cr; Department of Clinical Radiology, Salisbury District Hospital 11tr, 29tr, 51cr, 52cl, 52clb; Don Fawcett 15cr, 19tr; Dr Gary Settles 43bc; Dr. G. Moscoso

57tl; Dr. G. Oran Bredberg 22-23t; Dr. K. F. R. Schiller 48tc; Dr. P. Marazzi 47tl; Dr. Yorgas Nikas 56bl; Eye of Science 17tl, 35t, 48br; GCa/CNRI 16tr; Geoff Tompkinson 13ac; GJLP 17c; GJLP/CNRI 13br; J. C. Revy 27tr, 39tr, 62; James King-Homes 58tr; John Bavosi 42cl; Juergen Berger, Max-Planck Institute 38-39, 63; K. H. Kjeldsen 39br; Ken Eward 40b, 47b; Manfred Kage 45cl; Matt Meadows, Peter Arnold Inc 24bc; Mehau Kulyk 13c, 18tl, 21tr, 40tr; National Cancer Institute 4bl, 30-31; NIBSC 39br; Petit Format/Prof. E. Symonds 57tr; Philippe Plailly 28cr, 29bc; Prof. P. M. Motta, G. Macchiarelli, S.A Nottola 54-55t, ß61tr; Prof. P. Motta/ A.Caggiati/ University La Sapienza, Rome 22br; Prof. P. Motta/Dept of Anatomy/ University "La Sapienza"

Rome 5b, 10cra, 15tl, 21cr, 25tr, 25b, 36tr, 36-37, 40cr, 40cr, 51tr, 51b, 55tl, 55tr; Professors P. M. Motta and S. Makabe 56cr; Professors P.M. Motta & A. Gaggiati 23br; Quest 5cr, 6-7b, 21cr, 26ca, 37tl, 47ca, 47cr, 49bl, 53br; Salisbury District Hospital 60-61b; Scott Camazine 6tr, 26tl; Secchi-Lecaque/Roussel-UCLAF 24crb; Simon Fraser 4l, 5r; Stephen Gerard 8tl; Wellcome Dept of Cognitive Neurology 17r.

Book Jacket credits:

gettyone stone: back r; Paul Dance back cr; Spike Walker back l; **Science Photo Library:** CNRI back cl; Mehau Kulyk inside back, front; NIBSC inside front.